STEWARDING
YOUR
BEST
LIFE

The Biblical Key to
Personal, Relational and
Professional Success

SHERILYN HAMON-MILLER

Parsons Publishing House

Melbourne, Florida USA

Stewarding Your Best Life—The Biblical Key to Personal, Relational and Professional Success
by Sherilyn Hamon-Miller

Parsons Publishing House
P. O. Box 410063
Melbourne, FL 32941
www.ParsonsPublishingHouse.com
Info@ParsonsPublishingHouse.com

All Scripture quotations, unless otherwise indicated, are taken from *The Holy Bible, King James Version*, Cambridge, 1769.

Scripture quotations marked (NKJV) are taken from the *New King James Version*® (NKJV). Copyright © 1982 by Thomas Nelson, Inc. Used by permission. All rights reserved.

Scripture quotations marked (NIV) are taken from the *Holy Bible, New International Version*®, NIV®. Copyright © 1973, 1978, 1984 by Biblica, Inc.™ Used by permission of Zondervan. All rights reserved worldwide. www.zondervan.com.

Scripture quotations marked (ESV) are taken from *The Holy Bible: English Standard Version*, copyright 2001, Wheaton: Good News Publishers. Used by permission. All rights reserved.

Scripture quotations marked (NASB) are taken from the *New American Standard Bible*, Copyright 1960, 1962, 1963, 1971, 1972, 1973, 1975, 1977, 1995 by The Lockman Foundation. Used by permission.

Scripture quotations marked (NLT) are taken from the *Holy Bible, New Living Translation*, copyright 1996. Used by permission of Tyndale House Publishers, Inc., Wheaton, Illinois 60189. All rights reserved.

Scripture quotations marked (MSG) are taken from *THE MESSAGE*, copyright © 1993, 1994, 1995, 1996, 2000, 2001, 2002 by Eugene H. Peterson. Used by permission of Nav Press. All rights reserved. Represented by Tyndale House Publishers, Inc.

Cover Art: Rebecca Francis

ISBN-13: 978-1-60273-117-2
ISBN-10: 1-60273-117-9
Printed in the United States of America.
For World-Wide Distribution.

WHAT PEOPLE ARE SAYING

In *Stewarding Your Best Life*, Sherilyn Hamon-Miller unlocks the richness of God's generous blessings available to every believer through simply aligning with His prescribed plans, processes, and perspectives. This practical, yet powerful, book shines the light of God's truth upon our lives enabling us to be fruitful, productive, and fulfilled as good stewards of all He has entrusted us with. This message will challenge you, charge you, and change you and will also open the windows of blessings from heaven over your life and all you put your hands to do.

—APOSTLE JANE HAMON
PASTOR, VISION CHURCH
SANTA ROSA BEACH, FL

This book, *Stewarding Your Best Life*, will give you the wisdom to manage your life for God's special purpose bringing the greatest fulfillment and eternal rewards to you as you impact your spheres of influence for good. It will make sure you hear on that day, "Well done, good and faithful servant." Bless you Sherilyn for blessing God's children.

—DR. MELODYE HILTON
LEADERSHIP CONSULTANT/EXECUTIVE COACH
HILTON CONSULTING, LLC

Stewarding Your Best Life is a wonderful guide to becoming a success the way God wants you to. Sherilyn Hamon-Miller uses her own experiences and scriptural principles to lead you to a place of true service to God and His Kingdom. Sherilyn has lived "stewarding her best life" and uses her stories and humor to help you digest these important life lessons. Every believer should read this book.

—**DR. TIM HAMON**
CEO, CHRISTIAN INTERNATIONAL
SANTA ROSA BEACH, FL

Sherilyn Hamon-Miller has written a supernaturally practical book. It is full of pearls of wisdom that build character and success. I highly enjoyed it and felt God giving me strength to "finish well."

—**DR. CINDY JACOBS**
GENERALS INTERNATIONAL
RED OAK, TX

Stewarding Your Best Life gives you the right heart attitude to establish personal responsibility in every area of your life. There is also a call to holiness and authentic relationship with God that will cause you to prosper even as your soul prospers. Sherilyn's life is proof that to steward our souls, we must learn to love and forgive others.

—**DR. SHARON STONE**
FOUNDER, CHRISTIAN INTERNATIONAL EUROPE
UNITED KINGDOM

ACKNOWLEDGMENTS

I would like to thank those who have been a blessing and support in my life and in the writing of this book.

Thank you to my family. You have always been a support and a blessing to me in the good times and in the more difficult times of my life. You have helped me to grow and learn the keys I am sharing in this book.

First, I would like to acknowledge my parents, Dr. Bill and Evelyn Hamon. My mom went to be with Jesus on September 22, 2014; I miss her every day. I love you both very much and literally would not be here today without your love and support. You have been an example to me and so many around the world of stewarding a godly life. You have been willing to run the race and go through the process to be Christ-like in every area of your life.

My big brothers and their wives, Tim and Karen Hamon and Tom and Jane Hamon. I could not ask for more supportive, kind, caring, and loving siblings.

The loves of my life: my children and their spouses. Charity and her husband Joshua Agney. You are a godly, strong, loving, beautiful woman and my best girlfriend. My sons and their spouses, Joshua Miller and his wife Brooke, Daniel Miller and his wife Heather, and Joseph Miller. You are godly, strong, loving, and handsome men. I love all my children more than words can say. I am so proud of each and every one of you. We have been through a lot together, and you have always stood with me in every season of life—when we were rejoicing and when we were weeping. It is an honor to be your mother.

Last, but definitely not least, my amazing grandchildren: Atreya, Serenity, AJ, Milo, and Oliver. I am so blessed to have each and every one of you in my life. Gramma loves you very much.

Many thanks to Rebecca Francis. You were such a huge help in writing this book. It probably would not have been written without you. Thank you to Wendy Anderson for editing the book. Thank you to Darrell and Diane Parsons of Parsons Publishing House for taking a chance on a first-time author and publishing my book.

TABLE OF CONTENTS

THE HAMON FAMILY

Center: Bishop Bill Hamon. Back Row (left to right): Sherilyn Hamon-Miller, Jane Hamon, Tom Hamon, Tim Hamon, and Karen Hamon.

FOREWORD
by Bishop Bill Hamon
Bishop of Christian International Apostolic-Global Network

Sherilyn has presented some vital truths within this book that will help you live a more victorious life where it counts—in pleasing God.

I have watched her progress through many experiences during her lifetime. She has learned the truths written mainly from wisdom gained through life experiences. She has had plenty. She was raised in a minister's home and also pastored for ten years with her husband. When they left pastoring, Sherilyn traveled with her husband and children in full-time ministry. She has a ministry of her own, a combination of her father and mother's ministry, but with her unique style.

Everyone needs more wisdom and understanding in the ways of God and how to live a life that is pleasing to God. You will be more knowledgeable and an effective Christian when you finish reading this book.

I highly recommend this book to everyone who wants a closer relationship with Jesus Christ. These are practical truths that will help you with your daily Christian life. They will also help in your relationships with people in all walks of life. Read with confidence knowing that all you will read has been proven to be workable and productive in the life of a Christian.

Bless you, Sherilyn, for taking the time to write the wonderful truths in this book! May you continue to produce much more, as you demonstrate what it means to be a good and faithful servant through your own life.

Bill Hamon books include: *Your Highest Calling*; *The Eternal Church*; *Prophets & Personal Prophecy*; *Prophets & the Prophetic Movement*; *Prophets, Pitfalls, & Principles*; *Apostles/Prophets & the Coming Moves of God*; *The Day of the Saints*; *Who Am I & Why Am I Here*; *Prophetic Scriptures Yet to be Fulfilled*; *70 Reasons for Speaking in Tongues*; *How Can These Things Be?*; and *God's Weapons of War.*

PREFACE

I am confident by the time you finish reading this book, you will have a new understanding of what it is to be a good and faithful servant and a wise steward. You will know that God is in control of every aspect of your life. You will understand what it takes to hear those words "well done, good and faithful servant!"

I was raised in a Christian home, and my dad is a minister. When I was three years old, we lived on a Bible college campus where my dad taught. When I was eight years old, my Dad started Christian International and traveled in full-time ministry. I got married at 19 years old and became a pastor and then traveled in ministry as a wife and mother from 29 to 39 years old. I now work for Christian International with my dad full-time. So, I'm still in ministry. All that is to say I have been around a lot of ministers and Christians in my life. I have seen many mighty men and women of God who were full of integrity and lived to be Christ-like to the best of their abilities. I have also seen some mighty men and women of God who seemed to lead double lives, one way on the platform and another in their personal everyday lives. This contrast made me begin to wonder about the Scripture in Matthew 7:21-23:

> Not every one that saith unto me, Lord, Lord, shall enter into the kingdom of heaven; but he that doeth the will of my Father which is in heaven. Many will say to me in that day, Lord, Lord, have we not prophesied in thy name? and in thy name have cast out devils? and in thy name done many wonderful works? And then will I profess unto them, I never knew you: depart from me, ye that work iniquity.

This verse describes people who prophesied and cast out demons, but who don't make it into heaven. If you know Church history, you know that in the time since the book of Acts, Christians at large have only had the revelation of doing these things for a little over 100 years. For example, this Scripture really couldn't apply to Christians during the Middle Ages, most of whom were still paying penance for salvation, not casting out demons in Jesus' name. It has to apply to us today who have that revelation. It also couldn't apply to the vast majority of today's churches that don't believe in prophecy or deliverance. So actually there's only a select few of us who even have the potential to hear, "Depart from me… I never knew you."

Well, that's sobering. It got me thinking, What does it really take to hear "well done"? If you're already living a

Christian life, maybe even the life of a minister, then like me you're in the perfect place to ask this question. We need to know exactly what God is measuring, how to allow Him to measure us, and how to take inventory of our whole lives. We need to know how to look deeper, past the obvious issues of sin or salvation, into the fullness of what God wants us to accomplish during our time on the earth.

I've seen firsthand how a person can live an excellent ministry life—preaching, prophesying, and fulfilling his or her destiny in the area of ministry—without being a good steward of other parts of his or her life. It's shocking to some, but the truth is we can focus so much on what everyone else sees us doing that we forget to let God measure what He sees.

My questions about these Scriptures and what I've witnessed firsthand in people's lives are what inspired me to dig deeper. I wanted to know for myself where I stand with God on everything, not just on some things. And I'm glad I did! Some amazing things have happened since I started this journey.

For one thing, the answer to these questions showed me how important each of our parts are in the big picture. I come from a family of ministers who are well-known worldwide. Yet I'm not a well-known minister. I don't really travel or speak. But I've learned that my job is just as important. In fact, they couldn't do their jobs if I didn't do mine—so maybe mine is more important? (Just kidding of course!) Our jobs are equally important to God. What's most important, though, is how we steward or manage all of our lives, not just our jobs or ministries.

If you've felt insignificant, or if some parts of your life prosper while other parts don't, or even if you've been wildly successful by some outward appearance, it's time to ask this question for yourself.

When you learn the answer, you'll produce more fruit, you'll gain confidence knowing what God is asking of you, and you'll be prepared to have a "good and faithful" and "wise" response to every area of your life.

I hope, after your journey through this book, you will find the greatest validation you've ever had as you joyfully embrace your part in the Body of Christ!

Chapter 1

MEASURING SUCCESS

Do you ever wonder if you're doing enough?

People generally want to succeed. Few of us would say we want to fail or even to do the least possible with our lives. In order to keep track of our successes, we often use conventional measures. We might measure by looking ahead to milestones: marriage, children, ministry, retirement. Or we might look for markers along the way: promotions, awards, purchases, savings, happiness. No matter what we're measuring or how we are measuring it, most of our motives are all similar: we just want to do our best. Hopefully, we even want to please God.

But how can we know if we're doing our best?

THE TALE OF TWO ROBOTS

Let me start by telling you a story of a man who built a robot. This robot was human-like in every way. The man looked at the robot when he was finished and said, "I did a really good job." He charged the robot, and it came to life. The man was very happy. The robot worked and helped the man manage the area around him, and they would talk and fellowship. The man gave the robot a manual and said:

> Study this manual, know it inside and out, memorize it, and whatever you do, do not download new software. If you live by the manual and follow its instructions, you will work properly, and things will go well for you. Just know if you ever have any problems and need repair, I am here for you.

The robot took the manual and began to study it. Then one day the robot looked around and noticed he was the only robot. He asked his creator, "Could you build another robot for me to hang around with?" The man said, "Sure." So he did.

Things were going great until Robot #2 realized other technology existed that seemed to be more intelligent than the man. Robot #2 began to download and upgrade its software and told Robot #1, "This is great! You should do this too." But Robot #1 said, "It is not in the manual, and the man said, 'Whatever you do, do not download new software.' I'm not sure we should do this." Yet, Robot #2 convinced Robot #1 to download the new software.

Then the robots began to malfunction! They didn't know what was wrong. They were afraid to ask the man, because they knew he had said not to download the software. They tried to hide their malfunctions, but as soon as the man saw them, he realized they had caught a virus from the new download.

The robots were never quite the same. They continued to disobey the manual from time to time. Robot #1 decided it wanted to go swimming. But the manual said not to get wet or you will rust. But Robot #1 went anyway. Then the robot was stuck in the bottom of the ocean and was rusting. It was confused and said, "Why would the man make me so I can't swim? It is his fault not mine." Then it began to use its locator signal to call for the man to come and save it.

The man was a very forgiving and caring man and loved the robots he had created. So he got a boat and dive team and rescued the robot. Eventually, the robots began to understand the man who created them wrote the manual not to limit them, but to protect them and give them the best functioning existence they could have. As the robots began to remove the virus and repair the damage, they faithfully followed the manual. The man was then able to say to them, "You are wise managers and good and faithful servants."

God has given us a manual—the Bible. He has instructed us in the way we should live.

So what are we to do? We are to seek God constantly. We are to follow the Manual—Bible—that God has given us to live by and choose Him. "Choose you this day whom ye will serve" (Joshua 24:15).

Have you ever tried to put something together and not read the manual? When you get finished, it doesn't work correctly or it looks wrong? You have extra pieces or not enough? Then you read the manual and realize you could have saved yourself a lot of time and money if you had just read and followed the manual in the first place. That's how it is with following God's Word. When I meet my heavenly Father face to face, I want to hear Him say to me, "Well done, My good and faithful servant; you were a wise steward!" What about you?

IS WHAT WE DO FOR GOD ENOUGH?

What I'm about to say may go against everything inside of you. What we do in the natural and ministry for God is not enough to hear, "Well done, good and faithful servant." Now before you throw this book across the room, hear me out. God cares about the work of the ministry. He wants us to do it. He wants us to achieve wonderful things for His Kingdom. It's part of His plan. However, even when we do, it's not the only thing He measures.

The Bible tells us that simply preaching, casting out devils, prophesying, and doing wonderful works is not enough. Matthew 7:21-23 speaks of entering the kingdom of heaven:

> Not every one that saith unto me, Lord, Lord, shall enter into the kingdom of heaven; but he that doeth the will of my Father which is in heaven. Many will say to me in that day, Lord, Lord, have we not prophesied in thy name? and

in thy name have cast out devils? and in thy name done many wonderful works? And then will I profess unto them, I never knew you: depart from me, ye that work iniquity.

In this verse, the Lord literally sends Christian ministers away from heaven—away from Him. I believe that we can all agree that we do not want that to happen to us. When we get to heaven, we want God to say that we cast out devils in His name, prophesied in His name, did all these things in His name—and we want to enter into His Kingdom. We want to accomplish what He has called us to do.

So how do we change the last part of Matthew 7:21-23? How do we get Him to say, "Well done! Now enter in"? Matthew 25:21 gives us some insight: "His lord said unto him, Well done, thou good and faithful servant: thou hast been faithful over a few things, I will make thee ruler over many things: enter thou into the joy of thy lord." Therefore, when we are faithful over a few things, He will position us to rule over many things and to enter into the joy of the Lord. We want that. We want our portion.

ALLOWING GOD TO MEASURE

Being faithful over the "few things" is God's measure in Matthew 25. We'll talk more about some "few things" in later chapters. For now, let's talk about measuring. Are you ready for God to measure you? It might feel frightening, but allowing God to measure us now is one of the beauties of being here on earth. Part of our destiny on earth is to be conformed to the image of Christ.[1] This is an ongoing process all throughout our lives. We can always be more like Christ.

The Bible tells us God wants us to be conformed to the image of Christ, but it doesn't guarantee that just because we accept Jesus into our hearts that we will be conformed to His image. Scripture shows us that being renewed in our minds and walking in righteousness is a process.[2] It's not automatic. It doesn't happen once so that we never have to grow after that. This means, somehow, we have to be conformed. We participate. We have a role to play in the process.

So just what is our role? The good news is we do not have to measure ourselves. It is God who searches our hearts.[3] He knows us better than we know ourselves. But while we don't have to measure ourselves, we can submit to God's measuring process. His measuring process will reveal where we are and prepare us to progress more fully into Christ's image.

REVEALING WHERE WE ARE

Years ago my mom, Evelyn Hamon, wrote a powerful book about God's measuring process called *God's Tests Are Positive* (Christian International). She experienced God's testing at pivotal times in her life, and she learned how to recognize what was happening. More importantly, she learned to see testing in the positive light God intended it. In her book, she describes how we might think of testing as meaning "pass or fail." In God, testing isn't usually about passing or failing. Instead, it's about revealing where we are.

God's tests reveal what areas in our lives have been conformed to Christ so far, and what areas still need to conform.

The simplest difference between God's testing and our natural experience with testing is that God's tests look for progress, not perfection. The Scripture tells us to be perfect, but it also reminds us that even some of the greatest followers of Christ on earth never attained perfection. Paul the apostle said, "I don't mean to say that I have already achieved these things or that I have already reached perfection. But I press on to possess that perfection for which Christ Jesus first possessed me" (Philippians 3:12, NLT). So perfection itself couldn't possibly be God's measure—or you and I would have little chance! There is a difference between progressive perfection and ultimate perfection, like the difference between babyhood and maturity.

Progress is God's preferred measure. Did we progress with what we have? Did we do according to what we personally know to do? God holds us accountable for what He has given us. He expects us to act according to what we know: "Do not merely listen to the word, and so deceive yourselves. Do what it says" (James 1:22, NIV).

For me, that's liberating. I don't have to be responsible for anything God hasn't already done in me. And that's also enough. God's done a lot already. I've learned a lot in my lifetime. You probably have too! We have plenty to look at as a reflection and see whether or not we are being conformed to the image of Christ. As we are measured and found faithful by God, we will receive the promises He has for us.

PROMISES HAVE CONTINGENCIES

God made a lot of promises to us in His Word. He keeps His promises. He is the same yesterday, today, and forever. However, His promises are not one-sided. The Bible is full of promises from God that have contingencies. One is found in Luke 12:42: "And the Lord said, who then is that faithful and wise steward, whom his Lord shall make ruler over his household, to give them their portion of meat in due season?" In later chapters, we'll talk more about some specific promises.

Most promises are preceded with an "if"—if we believe, if we are a wise steward, etc. In order for God to keep His Word, He has to honor both the promise and the contingency. He does not lie. When a promise is fulfilled in our lives, we can celebrate knowing we kept our end as well. God wants to fulfill the promises He has given us. He wants only the best for us. Jeremiah 29:11 says, "I know the plans I have for you...to give you hope and a future" (NIV). He desires only good for us!

Since He wants us to receive each promise from Him, He makes it possible by enabling us to fulfill our "contingency." That's actually a promise that doesn't come with a contingency—that He is our enabler! Let's look at some Scriptures:

"And God is able to make all grace abound toward you, that you, always having all sufficiency in all things, may have an abundance for every good work" (2 Corinthians 9:8, NKJV).

"Looking unto Jesus, the author and finisher of our faith" (Hebrews 12:2, NKJV).

"Now unto Him who is able to do exceedingly abundantly above all that we ask or think, according to the power that works in us" (Ephesians 3:20, NKJV).

His power works in us to do what He asks us to do! Isn't God good that He would make us able to do the things we must do to receive His promises? It only requires a simple choice on our part.

A SINGLE, SIMPLE CHOICE

We have a choice today. We can choose our own standards, or we can submit to God's process of conforming us to His image.

Pray this prayer with me:

Lord, today I choose life. I choose Your ways. I know that means You will measure me. You will search my heart and my actions. You will look for my response to You. I invite You to do that now. Conform me to the image of Your Son. Let me see all things working together for that purpose. And when the time comes, remind me of Your promise. Remind me of my responsibility. And remind me how good You are, working all things out and giving me Your power to become who You want me to be. In Jesus' name. Amen.

Endnotes:

[1]Romans 8:20.

[2]Romans 12:2; Philippians 2:12.

[3]Jeremiah 17:10; Psalm 139:23-24; Romans 8:27.

Chapter 2

WHAT IS GOOD?

I am so proud and blessed to be a mother. Each time I gave birth and saw my newborn child, I knew I had done a good thing. I know lots of women have children, but I had tried unsuccessfully for five years to have a child. I would cry each month when I knew I wasn't pregnant. I would cry at baby showers. I kept getting prophecies that I would have children. I said, "I don't want another prophecy about children. I want a child!" God is good; He gave me the desire of my heart and gave me four children.

Every time God worked in Genesis, He observed His own work and called it good.[4] It's kind of like He graded Himself. Since He is God, we know His work was perfect. So when God also observes His servants as "good"—the same "good" He called His own work—He means something other than "good enough." We might use the word "good" to mean just above average or acceptable. Or we might use it to refer to good behavior or righteousness.

However, God uses the word "good" to mean specific things.

The word "good" stems from the Greek word *agathos*, meaning good, right, clear, generous, better, useful, helpful, and pleasant.[5] This is how God thought of His own work, and it's what He wants out of our efforts too. Let's look deeper at this.

GENEROUS AND PLEASANT

Of all the definitions of "good," generous may be the most surprising. To be good, according to God, includes generosity. Generosity doesn't only have to do with money; it implies being lavish, giving extra. It is the same word found in Matthew 20:15: "Don't I have the right to do what I want with my own money? Or are you envious because I am generous?"[6] In this parable, the employer pays the same to one who worked only a couple hours as he does to the one who worked the whole day. Those who worked longer were upset, but the employer says he has the right to be generous. And he even calls the upset ones wicked because they despised his generosity!

At Christian International, we put on several events each year, which require long hours and hard work by our staff and volunteers. When it's time to encourage our staff members at the start of an event, we have motto of sorts: "Today, we have two jobs. Our first job is our job. Our second job is everything else." This is the heart of generosity. It looks past the bare minimum expectation. It counts the minimum as not enough, and looks for "everything else." God tells us to go above and beyond. Matthew 5:40-42 says:

And if anyone wants to sue you and take your shirt, hand over your coat as well. If anyone forces you to go one mile, go with them two miles. Give to the one who asks you, and do not turn away from the one who wants to borrow from you (NIV).

This is where we get the saying, "Go the extra mile."

I am blessed to have a father and an entire family who demonstrate this kind of generosity. My dad is one of the most generous people I know. If you met him in a parking lot, unless you knew his face, you'd never know he was the founder of a global organization. You'd probably see him hold the door open for someone, perhaps even someone he calls an "old guy" at his "young" age of 85!

When God created the heavens and earth, He was generous. He could have made everything plain, just to function at the bare minimum. Instead, He made creation beautiful. He could have made just one kind of flower, or one kind of fruit, but He made multiple of almost everything—different colors, types and smells. Much more than just enough. He made it smell good, taste good, and sound good. He made the good feelings of a refreshing breeze and cool water on a hot day. Everything He does is generous, and that's His expectation of our goodness as well.

Generosity can be seen as something being pleasant. For something to be pleasant is "extra." You can have a car that gets you to your destination, or you can have a car that drives smoothly, cushions you just right, and has great surround sound. That's pleasant. To us, maybe it is a bonus for something to be pleasant. To God, it's just part of good.

USEFUL, HELPFUL, BETTER

The word "good" in "good and faithful servant" is the same word when God saw that His work in the Garden of Eden was good. One aspect of that meaning includes proper functioning.

Have you ever thought about creation? Nothing in creation serves just one purpose. Nothing is wasted. Even waste has a use! Everything God created has multiple purposes. Take, for example, a tree. A tree literally does dozens of tasks. It cleans the air, provides oxygen, cools us off, helps the soil, buffers extreme weather, serves as a home for all sorts of creatures, and so much more.[7] That's just one item in all of creation! I think we can all agree trees are useful, helpful, and better.

When God looks for good in us, He looks for useful, helpful, and better. He looks to see that we improve upon what we have, using it to the best of our abilities. When God called Moses, He asked him, "What is that in your hand?" (Exodus 4:2, NIV). All Moses had was a walking stick. God expected him to make that walking stick useful! And God enabled him to do it. First Peter 4:10 says it like this: "As each one has received a gift, minister it to one another, as good stewards of the manifold grace of God" (NKJV). First Corinthians tells us:

> Just as a body, though one, has many parts, but all its many parts form one body, so it is with

Christ. For we were all baptized by one Spirit so as to form one body—whether Jews or Gentiles, slave or free—and we were all given the one Spirit to drink. Even so the body is not made up of one part but of many. Now if the foot should say, 'Because I am not a hand, I do not belong to the body,' it would not for that reason stop being part of the body. And if the ear should say, "Because I am not an eye, I do not belong to the body," it would not for that reason stop being part of the body. If the whole body were an eye, where would the sense of hearing be? If the whole body were an ear, where would the sense of smell be? But in fact God has placed the parts in the body, every one of them, just as he wanted them to be. If they were all one part, where would the body be? As it is, there are many parts, but one body. The eye cannot say to the hand, "I don't need you!" And the head cannot say to the feet, "I don't need you!" On the contrary, those parts of the body that seem to be weaker are indispensable, and the parts that we think are less honorable we treat with special honor. And the parts that are unpresentable are treated with special modesty, while our presentable parts need no special treatment. But God has put the body together, giving greater honor to the parts that lacked it, so that there should be no division in the body, but that its parts should have equal concern for each other. If one part suffers, every part suffers with it; if one part is honored, every part rejoices with it (1 Corinthians 12: 12-26, NIV).

We are all to be useful, helpful, and better. We all have a part to play. Better does not mean one part is more important than another or better than another. We are each striving to be better at the part God has given us to be useful and helpful with. If we are not good at our part, then others will suffer. But if we are good at what God has given us, everyone rejoices.

When Moses was born, the midwife was helpful and useful by not killing him at birth. His sister was helpful and useful by putting him in the river and following the basket, then suggesting Moses's mother as a nursemaid. His mother was good because she was willing to take her own child, nurse him, then give him back to Pharaoh's daughter for her to raise as her own. That must have been difficult for her. Aaron, his brother, was helpful and useful—a good man—because he was willing to speak for Moses. Because each of these were willing to be helpful, useful, better, pleasant, and generous in seemingly small tasks, Moses was able to do as God had instructed him and lead the Children of Israel out of Egypt.[8]

RIGHT AND CLEAR

Finally, "good" includes what is right. That seems obvious, doesn't it? However, it's worth discussing. Just because something has a good result doesn't make it good if it isn't also right. This is what people mean when they say, "The end doesn't justify the means."

In an effort to be profitable or useful, we can be tempted to cut corners, to accept "collateral damage." However, before we give in to such a temptation, we should seek the

Lord. He will always make a way for something to be profitable and right.

This is connected to the statement made in Romans 13:3 which says:

> For rulers hold no terror for those who do right, but for those who do wrong. Do you want to be free from fear of the one in authority? Then do what is right and you will be commended (NIV).

Clearly, right action is at the heart of being good. This means to be in line with the law—both God's and man's. We'll talk more about authority in the next chapter. Let's look at "good" in other Scriptures:

GOOD THROUGHOUT SCRIPTURE

This remarkable word "good" appears 382 times in the Old Testament and 247 times in the New Testament. It must be important to God. Looking at some other Scriptures helps us gather the heart of what God really means when He says "good."

> "If you, then, though you are evil, know how to give good gifts to your children, how much more will your Father in heaven give good gifts to those who ask him!" (Matthew 7:11, NIV).

> "'Why do you ask me about what is good?' Jesus replied. 'There is only One who is good. If you want to enter life, keep the commandments'" (Matthew 19:17, NIV).

"To those who by persistence in doing good seek glory, honor and immortality, he will give eternal life" (Romans 2:7, NIV).

"And we know that in all things God works for the good of those who love him, who have been called according to his purpose" (Romans 8:28, NIV).

"Do not be overcome by evil, but overcome evil with good" (Romans 12:21, NIV).

"And God is able to bless you abundantly, so that in all things at all times, having all that you need, you will abound in every good work" (2 Corinthians 9:8, NIV).

"Being confident of this, that he who began a good work in you will carry it on to completion until the day of Christ Jesus" (Philippians 1:6, NIV).

"Every good and perfect gift is from above, coming down from the Father of the heavenly lights, who does not change like shifting shadows" (James 1:17, NIV).

The highest and most important application of "good" to God, the Father, is that which applies to being conformed to the image of His Son, Jesus Christ. Jesus declared no one is good but God. Jesus was the expressed image of God, and "God manifest in the flesh" (1 Timothy 3:16). True goodness is only in God. So if we want to really be good, we need to pull on God's goodness to be alive and active in our lives. This will enable God to say, "Well done, **good** steward."

From just eight of the over 500 examples in the Bible, we can see that good means a lot to God. I want Him to be able to use that word to describe my life, don't you?

PRAYER AND ACTIVATION

Let's pray:

Lord, thank You for making me good according to Your Word. Thank You that, by Your grace, I am able to do what is right in Your eyes. Thank You also for causing me to be more than just "not wrong." Make me extravagantly good. Show me ways to demonstrate Your goodness. Show me good works You've prepared in advance for me to do. Give me Your heart of generosity! I choose the higher standard of Your goodness today, and I trust You to fulfill it in me. In Jesus' name. Amen.

Now let's do an activation. If you're not familiar with activations, let me explain. It means taking action on what we have learned or igniting something that is already in us. It means utilizing our faith with works. My dad coined this phrase about fifty years ago when he began teaching that we can "activate" the gifts of the Spirit inside of us (see ***Ministering Spiritual Gifts*[9]**). Follow the prompts below to activate seeing, receiving, and demonstrating God's goodness.

1.) Has God's goodness shown up in your life? List areas where you know God has done more than the minimum for you, where He has been generous, pleasant, useful, and right.

2.) Have you been demonstrating "goodness" the same way? List areas where you know you have gone above the minimum, made something pleasant, been generous, used your gifts to bless others, or demonstrated usefulness.

3.) Now ask God to show you an area where you may only be fulfilling the minimum. This could be an area of responsibility, a relationship, or somewhere you could step out, like volunteering. Write it down.

What is the simplest step you can take to improve in this area? Is it a step you can do today or this week at the latest? Make a plan now to act on doing good in this area the Lord has shown you. Then do it!

Endnotes:
[4]Genesis 1:10, 12, 18, 21, 25, 31.
[5]Packer, J.I. (1996). Good. In D. R. W. Wood, I. H. Marshall, A. R. Millard, and D.J. Wiseman (Eds.), New Bible Dictionary (3rd ed.) Leicester, England; Downers Grove, IL: InterVarsity Press.
[6]Swanson, J. (1997). Dictionary of Biblical Languages with Semantic Domains: Greek (New Testament) (electronic ed.). Oak Harbor: Logos Research Systems, Inc.
[7]How Trees Make a Difference—Trees for Wildlife | National Wildlife Federation. (n.d.). Retrieved August 20, 2018, from https://www.nwf.org/en/Trees-for-Wildlife/About/Trees-Make-a-Difference.
[8]Exodus2-4.
[9]Hamon, Bill. (1996). Ministering Spiritual Gifts. Santa Rosa Beach, FL: Christian International.

Chapter 3

WHAT IS FAITHFUL?

I work for my brother, Dr. Tim Hamon, as an employee. When I first started working for Christian International, Dr. Tim put me at the front desk answering phones. I was there for a while, and then he moved me to help in the Christian International Apostolic Network. I worked there for several months, maybe even a year, and then he moved me to the Ministry Training College. After several months, he moved me to the accounting department, then the media department. He kept moving me, after a period of time, to different departments. I got worried, thinking, I must be doing a really bad job, and he can't find a place to put me.

Despite my insecurities, I remained faithful in what my boss had told me to do to the best of my ability. I was sure he was going to come to me and say he didn't need me and couldn't find a place for me. But that wasn't what he was doing at all! He was training me in all the different areas of CI. Eventually, he moved me to the Administration Department. Now I am the Chief Operating Officer, a position I would never have been successful at if I had not learned about each of the various departments.

We all work for God, not for man, so we know our boss is always working all things for our good.You may feel as if God is moving and changing you. You get settled in one area, and then you are switched to another area in life. If you are faithful where God has you at the moment, in the small things, then you will be ruler over much and promotion will come.

What happens if a business fails? If I, as an employee, did my job well, where does the blame fall? If it falls apart, where does the blame fall? If the business does well, who gets the praise? In either scenario, who are we going to look to? The boss! If I'm faithful to do what my brother asks, as the boss, he's ultimately responsible for what I do and for the outcome, good or bad. Thank the Lord that He is the true boss, and His yoke is easy! God is the owner of everything. If we allow Him to be the boss of our lives, then He is responsible. But if we take control and are the boss of our lives, then we are responsible. I would prefer God to be the boss. "The earth is the Lord's, and everything in it, the world, and all who live in it" (Psalm 24:1, NIV).

God asks us to be faithful. We might hear most about faithfulness in regard to our relationship with Him and to our marriages. However, God asks it in everything that we do. The little things mean a lot to God. He may condemn those who are not faithful in the big things, like in their covenant with Him. But Scripture suggests that He rewards based on faithfulness to the little things.

Faithfulness is the word *pistos* meaning "reliable, faithful, believing, trustworthy, certain, true, observant of, and steadfast to one's trust. " It also means this:

- of persons who show themselves faithful in the transaction of business, the execution of commands, or the discharge of official duties.
- one who kept his plighted faith, worthy of trust.
- that can be relied on.

It's easy to see that faithfulness means more than not turning away from God. Faithfulness has a lot more to do with our everyday behavior and responsibilities. We'll talk about some specific daily behaviors in later chapters. Let's discuss what some of these qualities of faithfulness look like to us today.

BELIEVING

As I said, my brother is my boss. According to God, part of my being faithful as his employee includes my believing in him. Believing is an important part of faithfulness because it helps empower us to fulfill the rest of what faithfulness means.

This word believing, at the root of faithfulness, shows up in John 20:27: "Then he said to Thomas, 'Put your finger here; see my hands. Reach out your hand and put it into my side. Stop doubting and believe'" (NIV). "Believe" in this Scripture is the root word of faithfulness. In this context it means believing in God. Actually, it doesn't really even mean the kind of faith that is without any proof. It is more like being convinced with proof. Remember, Jesus was talking to "Doubting Thomas," the guy famous for not believing. He basically said, "When you touch My side, you'll believe. Then you'll be convinced—finally!"

To be faithful, we have to be convinced. Whether or not we have evidence, we have to believe. I have to be convinced that not only is my brother the boss at my workplace, but that God has put him in that position and he is worthy of my respect and faithfulness as his employee. Even if I think he isn't right on a certain matter, I can believe in his authority anyway. It's a choice I make. Even if I question his decision on a certain matter, even if I may think I know better, I choose to demonstrate faithfulness.

God wants us to believe, not just in Him but in the principle of authority He has given us. Now I know that some authority figures in this world are unrighteous and even evil. I am not saying that every boss, parent, teacher, government leader, etc., is doing a good job. Some are malfunctioning badly, like the robots from Chapter 1 when they weren't following the manual. But I am saying that the principle of authority comes from God: "Everyone must submit to governing authorities. For all authority comes from God, and those in positions of authority have been placed there by God" (Romans 13:1, NLT). Whether it's our workplace, our homes, the local laws, or any other areas we encounter authority, our job is to be convinced. They are the authority. Even if we think they don't know best, they are the authority, and believing in them is the foundation of being faithful.

> For I am a man under authority, having soldiers under me: and I say to this man, Go, and he goeth; and to another, Come, and he cometh; and to my servant, Do this, and he doeth it. When Jesus heard it, he marvelled, and said to them that followed, Verily I say unto you, I have not found so great faith, no, not in Israel (Matthew 8:9-10).

TRUE AND CERTAIN

"As a matter of honor, one man owes it to another to manifest the truth." —Thomas Aquinas

Another idea at the heart of faithfulness is being true and certain. This is the same root word found in Proverbs 14:5: "An honest witness does not deceive, but a false witness pours out lies" (NIV).[13] To be faithful, we need to be honest and truthful. It is one of the Ten Commandments: "Thou shall not lie" (Exodus 20:16).

When we are faithful, we don't merely accomplish a task. We accomplish it with integrity. We ask ourselves: was I honest? Did I keep accurate records?

When I was a bank teller, I learned just moving a decimal a little to the right or left could make a very big difference in the outcome of a deposit or withdrawal. Adding one little zero or taking away one little zero could make a big difference in other people's lives and finances. I had to be faithful in the smallest areas. I had to be faithful to make sure my cash drawer balanced every day. If I was off even by one cent, I would get written up. Not being faithful in the smallest of things can affect your life and others' lives.

Without complete truth, whatever we have is distorted. On our jobs, were we honest with our time sheets? If not, we may have fulfilled our tasks at work, but what we have is still distorted. I'm not saying this to be what some might call "legalistic." However, as the saying goes, "The devil is in the details." If we lack truth, it thwarts our efforts by giving room to the enemy.

> Therefore, putting away lying, "Let each one of you speak truth with his neighbor," for we are members of one another. "Be angry, and do not sin": do not let the sun go down on your wrath, nor give place to the devil. Let him who stole steal no longer, but rather let him labor, working with his hands what is good, that he may have something to give him who has need. Let no corrupt word proceed out of your mouth, but what is good for necessary edification, that it may impart grace to the hearers. And do not grieve the Holy Spirit of God, by whom you were sealed for the day of redemption. Let all bitterness, wrath, anger, clamor, and evil speaking be put away from you, with all malice. And be kind to one another, tenderhearted, forgiving one another, even as God in Christ forgave you" (Ephesians 4:25-32, NKJV).

To truly be faithful, first we must be truthful. Here's a few more Scriptures on truth:

"Send out your light and your truth; let them lead me; let them bring me to your holy hill and to your dwelling" (Psalm 43:3, ESV).

"O LORD, who shall sojourn in your tent? Who shall dwell on your holy hill? He who walks blamelessly and does what is right and speaks truth in his heart" (Psalm 15:1-2, ESV).

"These are the things that you shall do: Speak the truth to one another; render in your gates judgments that are true and make for peace" (Zechariah 8:16, ESV).

"Therefore, having put away falsehood, let each one of you speak the truth with his neighbor, for we are members one of another" (Ephesians 4:25, ESV).

TRANSACT AND EXECUTE

Now we're getting to the bottom line of faithfulness—our actions. Faithfulness isn't just a condition of our hearts. It's the end result—what we do based on the condition of our hearts. Faith without works is dead.[14] So is faithfulness. For faithfulness to be real, it means we transact and execute our commands and responsibilities.

I love my dad, Dr. Bill Hamon. I also respect him and honor him, and as you know, I work for my dad as well as my brother. But if all I do is love, respect, and honor my dad in my heart, does it matter? As his executive administrator, I manage his schedule. But if I were to just put a meeting on his calendar and never book his flight, hotel room, and so on, he would not make it to the meeting to equip God's people and do what God has called him to do. I manage his finances, but if I just collected the bills and didn't pay them or received the money and didn't deposit it, there would be no finances to buy the plane ticket and book the hotel so he could make it to his destination. When he comes home from a trip, I tell him I love him. But I still have to process his accounting. I may love him enough to spend my life serving him, but if I don't actually do what needs to be done, then I'm not being a faithful steward/manager or a wise servant. If I am unfaithful, that would affect my father's ability to minister to people all around the world. I believe I will get the same blessing and reward for being faithful in what God has called me to do as my dad will for being faithful in what God has called him to do.

Execution of tasks is the final result of faithfulness. It starts with believing and being honest, but it ends in behaving the way we are supposed to behave. I like this definition of faithfulness: "of persons who show themselves faithful in the transaction of business, the execution of commands, or the discharge of official duties."[15] I want to be that person. There's a few things this means: taking action, obeying, and knowing our responsibilities.

We can determine if we are being faithful by asking ourselves these questions:

- Am I obeying direct instructions I have been given?
- Do I know what I am supposed to be doing in addition to direct instructions?
- Am I taking action?

ACTIVATION

Pray this prayer with me, and then we will do an activation.

Lord, I desire a heart of faithfulness like You describe in Your Word. Fill my heart with Your truth. Fill me with belief in You and in all authority You've given me. Wherever necessary, help my unbelief. I surrender my actions to You. You are Lord of my life including everything I do. I commit to living in belief and truth and executing Your will in my life. Thank You that it's You who makes me able to do this. I receive Your grace to do it. In Jesus' name. Amen.

Now, I want to encourage you to take inventory of an area of your life right now. You can pick any area of your life where you have responsibility: work, family, your local church, etc. In any area of responsibility, we have two jobs: our job and everything else. That means our direct orders and those things that can be understood through common sense, wisdom, and understanding the culture around us.

1.) What are your direct instructions in this responsibility? Maybe they're from God or maybe from an earthly authority.

2.) What are a few things you are responsible to do that may not have been direct orders? You can find things like this in the Bible. We're all responsible to do every good work prepared in advance for us to do.[16]

3.) Is there any immediate action that needs to be taken? Have you been procrastinating? Are there any actions you dislike and, therefore, haven't been faithful with? If so, just surrender that to the Lord. Ask Him to help you with these tasks. I assure you He will! He wants to find you faithful as much as you want Him to.

Endnotes:
[10]Thomas, R. L. (1998). New American Standard Hebrew-Aramaic and Greek dictionaries : updated edition. Anaheim: Foundation Publications, Inc.
[11]Pistos—New Testament Greek Lexicon—King James Version. Retrieved from https://www.biblestudytools.com/lexicons/greek/kjv/pistos.html.
[12] (2011). The Lexham Analytical Lexicon to the Greek New Testament. Logos Bible Software.
[13](2012). The Lexham Analytical Lexicon of the Septuagint. Bellingham, WA: Lexham Press.
[14]James 2:20.
[15]Pistos—New Testament Greek Lexicon—King James Version. Retrieved from https://www.biblestudytools.com/lexicons/greek/kjv/pistos.html.
[16]Ephesians 2:10.

Chapter 4

WHAT IS WISE?

I heard a funny saying: "I don't like to think before I speak; I like to be as surprised as everyone else." This has been something I have had to work on! But the Bible says to let every man be swift to hear, slow to speak, and slow to wrath.[17] I'm learning it is better to think before I speak.

You'd think it would be enough to follow the rules. If I obey God and do what I know is right, won't I be blessed? Won't everything work out for me? Well, maybe not the way we think of it. Yes, if we belong to God, everything will work for our good.[18] Of course it will. But that doesn't mean we'll have every good thing God wants to give us. There are some good things God has for us that we can't get by obeying commandments. No. The only way to receive certain things from God is to excel in something else: wisdom.

Jesus said it like this: "And the Lord said, who then is that faithful and wise steward, whom his Lord shall make ruler over his household, to give them their portion of meat in due season?" (Luke 12:42).

OK, I get the faithful part. All Christians know we're supposed to be faithful. But apparently faithful isn't enough to get the best from the Master. Each of us must be a faithful and wise steward to receive God's promise of our portion. Not only that, but we will also get the promise of being made rulers.[19] When Jesus returns, He wants to find us being faithful and wise managers of what He has put us in charge of. If He does, it will be good for us.

God likes wisdom. Hey, I like wisdom too! I like it when people around me have wisdom. I especially like when my kids have wisdom. I like when they face a problem and solve it—when they don't waste—when they think through the consequences of their actions. And how I feel about my kids having wisdom could give me a clue about how God feels about me having wisdom. "A wise son brings joy to his father, but a foolish son brings grief to his mother" (Proverbs 10:1, NIV).

So what is wisdom to God?

GOD'S DEFINITION OF WISDOM

To be wise in Luke 12:42 means to be "prudent, sensible, and mindful of one's interests."[20] It is the Greek word *phronimos*, and it includes ideas like being "shrewd in the management of practical affairs"[21]—being discreet and making provision for the future. Jesus used this word in Matthew. The English translations give further insight to its meaning:

> "Therefore everyone who hears these words of Mine
> and acts on them, may be compared to a wise man
> who built his house on the rock"
> (Matthew 7:24, NASB).

> "Behold, I send you out as sheep in the midst of wolves;
> so be shrewd as serpents and innocent as doves"
> (Matthew 10:16, NASB).

> "Five of them were foolish, and five were prudent...but
> the prudent took oil in flasks along with their lamps"
> (Matthew 25:2, 4, NASB).

This word only appears a few times in the entire New Testament. Let's look at what Jesus means when He uses it.

DOING, NOT JUST HEARING

The first time this word appears in the Bible is Matthew 7:24 (above), when Jesus says that someone is wise for building their house on the rock. He says that's the kind of wisdom we have when we hear His words and act on them. So being wise includes doing what you have heard.

Let's look at how important hearing and doing are. James says, "But be doers of the word, and not hearers only, deceiving yourselves" (James 1:22, ESV). If we hear the Word—Jesus' words—and we don't do it, we deceive ourselves. Deception is the result of hearing and not doing.

Wisdom includes being free of deception. If we have wisdom, we'll do what we know. We won't lie to ourselves or make excuses about why we aren't doing what we know and what we have heard from the Lord.

CLEVER, DISCERNING AWARENESS

The second time this word for wise appears is in Matthew 10:16 (quoted earlier) where Jesus tells us how to protect ourselves against wolves. He says be "shrewd as serpents." Here, it means "clever discerning awareness."[22] Of course Jesus combines this type of wisdom with innocence so that we never use it destructively. But it's a pretty sharp kind of wisdom. It's not just the kind of wisdom that keeps you from touching a hot stove. It's the same wisdom that the serpent in the Garden had, the serpent who was "crafty":

> Now the serpent was more crafty than any of the wild animals the Lord God had made. He said to the woman, "Did God really say, 'You must not eat from any tree in the garden'?" (Genesis 3:1, NIV).

The serpent discerned the weakness in Eve. He found the hole in her resolve using his craftiness. His intent was obviously evil, but you could say it was his "discernment" that enabled him to be so good at being evil.

God wants us to have clever, discerning awareness, just like the serpent had. When we combine that with innocence, our discernment will help us see the weak places that need strength. It will help us build each other up, fill gaps, and bring restoration.

PRACTICALLY APPLIED WISDOM

The last place Jesus uses this word for wise is in the parable of the ten virgins. Here five of them were foolish and five were prudent. The prudent ones brought oil in their lamp for the long journey (Matthew 25, quoted earlier).

In this example, wise refers to practical wisdom. Today we call it "street smarts." The story shows us what practical wisdom looks like. The five prudent virgins either knew they were leaving their homes for a long time, or they didn't know how long they were leaving. Either way, they thought ahead and brought extra oil just in case. They were prepared for the future. They took a look at their situation and then thought ahead.

Live your life like you may die tomorrow, but plan your life like you will live to be 100. This is how a wise person lives.

Today it would be like leaving the house without an umbrella on a day it might rain. Sure when you first leave your house, it isn't raining. But you can look at the sky, or feel the air, or look up the weather forecast for the day, and then you'll know what you need to be prepared for. Practically applied wisdom might be what my mom calls common sense. It's just common sense to take an umbrella if it there's a chance of rain.

Practical wisdom protects us from avoidable problems. It's like God is saying, *"Don't be dumb, OK? It will really help you!"* I can't tell how many times I could have avoided getting soaked in the rain if I had just brought an umbrella. Whether big or small, avoidable mishaps are challenging because they were avoidable in the first place. You can't prepare for everything, but you can prepare for what you know is likely to happen. That is common sense. In making a decision, common sense is knowing:

- Who (to talk to or connect with).
- When (when to talk to or connect with that person).
- Where (where to talk to or connect with that person).
- How (how to talk or connect with that person).
- What (thinking through what the outcome will be).

That's practical wisdom. That's prudence.

GOD'S EMPHASIS ON WISDOM

Hopefully you've caught on by now that wisdom is important to God. Let's look deeper at just how important it is. This verse describes how beautiful wisdom is:

> Blessed is the one who finds wisdom, and the one who gets understanding, for the gain from her is better than gain from silver and her profit better than gold. She is more precious than jewels, and nothing you desire can compare

with her. Long life is in her right hand; in her
left hand are riches and honor. Her ways are
ways of pleasantness, and all her paths are peace
(Proverbs 3:13-18, ESV).

Long life. Riches. Honor. Pleasantness. Peace. These are
the jewels at the end of the wisdom road. We're not
actually guaranteed all these things, but wisdom can help
us achieve them in God. He has long life and riches and
so much more for us on the other side of wisdom.

Get wisdom, get understanding; do not forget
my words or turn away from them. Do not
forsake wisdom, and she will protect you; love
her, and she will watch over you. The
beginning of wisdom is this: Get wisdom.
Though it cost all you have, get understanding.
Cherish her, and she will exalt you; embrace
her, and she will honor you. She will give you a
garland to grace your head and present you
with a glorious crown (Proverbs 4:5-9, NIV).

I couldn't say it better myself. Get wisdom! I hope you
realize this means we don't automatically have it. I wish
we did. I wish I did. I'd love to see myself and my loved
ones and my staff all have an extra dose of wisdom.

James 1:5 says, "If any of you lacks wisdom, let him ask of
God, who gives to all liberally and without reproach, and
it will be given to him" (NKJV). It's possible for believers
to lack wisdom, but it's also possible to ask for it and get
it. When you are a child you have some wisdom, but as
you are instructed by your parents, you learn more

wisdom. As you go to school, you get knowledge which leads to more wisdom and a higher understanding. We don't judge a child and say he or she is not wise because they don't have the wisdom we have. They must get wisdom. We wouldn't put a child in a management or leadership position until he or she has matured and proven himself to be good, wise, and faithful.

By the way, this verse appears just before the one that says if we hear the Word and don't do it, we deceive ourselves. James was on a roll! The entire first chapter of James is filled with wisdom. I encourage you to read it.

The more wisdom we have, the more of its characteristics we will show.

CHARACTERISTICS OF WISDOM

Humble
Humility is a characteristic of wisdom. Not only that, but it also produces wisdom!

> "When pride comes, then comes disgrace, but with humility comes wisdom" (Proverbs 11:2, NIV).

Thoughtful About What You Say
How's this for a twist? Even if you're not wise, you can be wise by not speaking!

> "The one who has knowledge uses words with restraint, and whoever has understanding is even-tempered. Even fools are thought wise if they keep silent, and discerning if they hold their tongues" (Proverbs 17:27-28, NIV).

Not Reacting with Emotion

That verse in Proverbs 17 mentions being "even-tempered." In a moment when we have intense feelings, we can also have wisdom if we choose restraint.

"A fool vents all his feelings, but a wise man holds
them back" (Proverbs 29:11, NKJV).

Teachable

Another quality of wisdom is being teachable. If you can receive instruction from another person, take advice, seek counsel, and listen to a rebuke, you've got wisdom.

"Where there is strife, there is pride, but wisdom is found
in those who take advice" (Proverbs 13:10, NIV).

"Listen to counsel and receive instruction, that you may
be wise in your latter days" (Proverbs 19:20, NKJV).

"A wise son heeds his father's instruction, but a scoffer
does not listen to rebuke" (Proverbs 13:1, NKJV).

And So Much More!

As if all these aren't enough great qualities that come from wisdom, here's a remarkable verse that gives us the cherry on top of our wisdom sundae:

"But the wisdom that is from above is first pure,
then peaceable, gentle, willing to yield, full of mercy and
good fruits, without partiality and without hypocrisy"
(James 3:17, NKJV).

Wow, really? I can honestly say I don't think of this verse as my go-to wisdom verse. I usually find myself in

Proverbs for that. But what a perfect picture of wisdom! It's so much more than "smarts." It's a major part of the nature of God.

So let's read the verse about the "wise steward" with our new understanding of what all it really means:

> And the Lord said, who then is that faithful and wise, [humble, teachable, receiving instruction, listening to rebuke, thoughtful of what they say, not reacting in anger, pure, peaceable, gentle, willing to yield, full of mercy and good fruits, without partiality, without hypocrisy] steward, whom his Lord shall make ruler over his household, to give them their portion of meat in due season? (Luke 12:42).

Can we say these qualities exist in our lives? Let's be the ones who are made rulers over our Lord's household by choosing (and getting more) wisdom.

PRAYER AND ACTIVATION

Lord, You said if anyone lacks wisdom, to ask You who will give it freely. Today I am asking for more wisdom. Give me wisdom to please You in every area of my life. I want to be a doer of Your Word, to have clever, discerning awareness and to demonstrate all the qualities of wisdom. I yield to You so that I can be conformed into Your image of humility, thoughtfulness, being even-tempered, and being teachable. I am willing to be made like You in wisdom. In Jesus' name. Amen.

Now, in your own words, ask God to give you an opportunity to obey His voice today. The Bible says the fear of the Lord is the beginning of wisdom, and as we saw above, being a doer of His Word is critical. When you ask the Lord for an opportunity to obey His voice today, believe that He will lead you. He will bring to your remembrance this prayer, quicken your spirit to recognize His voice, and make a divine opportunity for you to act on what He shows you.

Endnotes:
[17]James 1:19.
[18]Romans 8:28.
[19]Romans8:17; 2 Timothy 2:12.
[20]Thomas, R. L. (1998). New American Standard Hebrew-Aramaic and Greek dictionaries : updated edition. Anaheim: Foundation Publications, Inc.
[21]Merriam-Webster, I. (2003). Merriam-Webster's collegiate dictionary. (Eleventh ed.). Springfield, MA: Merriam-Webster, Inc.
[22]Merriam-Webster, I. (1996). Merriam-Webster's collegiate thesaurus. Springfield, MA: Merriam-Webster.

Chapter 5

STEWARDS AND SERVANTS

I owned a yogurt shop for about three years. I was the boss. It was kind of cool when I first started to be the boss. I had employees. I was in charge.

But then something changed. The business started struggling financially. It wasn't as nice any longer. When there wasn't much money, I still had to pay the employees. Once the business started going down, I had to put my own money into it to keep paying those employees. They didn't care. Maybe they didn't even know. But it wasn't their responsibility. I was the owner. The buck stopped with me, as they say.

The opposite is true in the kingdom of God. In the Kingdom, we don't own anything. We're not the boss of anything. We don't own ourselves, our families, our possessions, our ministries, or our careers. Nothing. We'll talk more later about just how little belongs to us, but for now let's talk about being a manager. That's what we really are: managers of God's affairs.

MANAGING GOD'S FAMILY AFFAIRS

The word "steward" in Luke 12 is the word *oikonomos*: "And the Lord said, who then is that faithful and wise steward, whom his Lord shall make ruler over his household, to give them their portion of meat in due season?" (Luke 12:42).

This word for steward means one who manages the affairs of a household; it's especially a "manager to whom the head of the house has entrusted the management of his affairs, the care of receipts and expenditures, and the duty of dealing out the proper portion to every servant and children not yet of age."[23] It's a lot like a manager in a modern-day workplace, except its more personal.

I think it's interesting that Jesus chose to talk about someone in charge of a personal household rather than something less personal, like a business. It's not like Jesus didn't know what a business was; He could have used a word that means business owner. Yet, He chose this word to talk about managing in the Kingdom because the Kingdom is personal to God. The Kingdom is about His family. It's His household.

God is our heavenly Father. We all know that. We know it from the Lord's Prayer, "Our Father in Heaven." We know it because Jesus is the firstborn of all our brothers. We know it because God refers to us as His sons and daughters throughout Scripture. So when God calls us stewards, He means managers of His family, the Body of Christ, and all that concerns it:

> If ye then, being evil, know how to give good gifts unto your children: how much more shall your heavenly Father give the Holy Spirit to them that ask him? (Luke 11:13).

Our Father God is a good Father. He wants to bless us. He gave us the Holy Spirit and His Word as tools so we can manage well. God wants us to succeed. He wants His children to succeed. Many times, we look at Father God as a judge who wants us to fail, but God is a good father who wants good and success for us, just as we want success for our children. He wants us to manage His family well. Imagine that! We are all responsible for the affairs of God's family

The word used in Matthew 25 is "servant":

> His lord said unto him, Well done, good and faithful servant; thou hast been faithful over a few things, I will make thee ruler over many things: enter thou into the joy of thy lord (Matthew 25:23).

This word "servant" means "one who is in permanent relation of servitude to another, his will altogether consumed in the will of the other."[24] There you go. A servant has no will of his or her own. A real servant is consumed with the will of the one being served.

How do we manage then? We seek the will of the Father. It's not our will; it's not what we want. It's what He wants. Jesus said, "O my Father, if it be possible, let this cup pass from me: nevertheless not as I will, but as thou wilt" (Matthew 26:39).

We can know God's will. It's in the Manual. He wrote the Manual. He gave us the Manual. Now it's up to us to seek it, learn it, and use it.

> Then Jesus answered and said verily verily I say unto you, the Son can do nothing of Himself, but what He seeth the Father do. For what things so ever He doeth, these also doeth the son likewise (John 5:19).

So what are we supposed to do? We do as Jesus did, and we do the will of the Father.

MANAGEMENT, THE FIRST JOB ON EARTH

When God created Adam and Eve, from the beginning He set them up as good stewards (managers) to name all the animals and work the garden. They understood it all belonged to God. They knew they were just there to manage and be faithful servants over what God had given them to manage. He made rules for them to follow: do not eat from the tree of the knowledge of good and evil, have dominion, be fruitful, and multiply. They had specific instructions from God, then the rest was up to them to manage well.

The Bible gives us many examples of those who proved themselves to be good managers of their time, families, money, bodies, or thoughts. Jesus proved Himself to be a good carpenter, faithful to His earthly father, and a good steward of earthly and heavenly responsibilities. Abraham proved himself by leaving his home and family to obey God, then being willing to sacrifice his own promised son. Jacob was good at his trade and faithful to it. Joseph proved himself to be a good household servant in Potiphar's house. Then he was a good prisoner and supervisor in prison, and later he was a good right-hand to the pharaoh. Ruth proved to be a good daughter-in-law to Naomi. David proved himself to be a good son and shepherd, even a good errand boy, before proving himself to be a good manager of the armies of Israel and finally all of Israel.

Most great leaders of the Bible were proven faithful in multiple areas or occasions. All of them went through many difficult situations, trials, and tribulations, and all had some failures—except Jesus—yet, overall they stayed faithful. Good management, proven through testing, has always been a priority to God:

> Let a man so account of us, as of the ministers
> of Christ and stewards of the mysteries of God.
> Moreover it is required in stewards, that a man
> be found faithful (1 Corinthians 4:1-2).

"His Lord said unto him, well done good and faithful servant; thou hast been faithful over a few things, I will make you ruler over many things; enter thou into the joy of the Lord" (Matthew 25:21).

"The refining pot is for silver and the furnace for gold,
But the LORD tests hearts" (Proverbs 17:3, NASB).

> In this you greatly rejoice, even though now for
> a little while, if necessary, you have been
> distressed by various trials, so that the proof of
> your faith, being more precious than gold
> which is perishable, even though tested by fire,
> may be found to result in praise and glory and
> honor at the revelation of Jesus Christ (1 Peter
> 1:6-7, NASB).

Remember, He is making us into His image. Only
someone with His image can really manage His family
affairs well. He is looking for people who can rule and
reign with Him in eternity, not just who make it into
heaven by the skin of their teeth: "For whom he did
foreknow, he also did predestinate to be conformed to the
image of his Son, that he might be the firstborn among
many brethren" (Romans 8:29).

"But we all, with open face beholding as in a glass the
glory of the Lord, are changed into the same image from
glory to glory" (2 Corinthians 3:18).

A LIGHT BURDEN

I no longer own a yogurt shop. I'm not the boss anymore.
Now, I'm almost never the boss actually. There's always
someone right above me. If I do what is asked of me and
it doesn't work out, someone above me faces the
consequences. That makes my burden much lighter. The
boss has the greatest burden on his shoulders.

That's why the Word says the government is on Jesus' shoulders. Our burden is easy. It's light. You know why? Because He's in charge. He's the boss. We're just managers. We're just here to manage what He's given us to manage. The buck stops with Him. If we do our part in what He gives us, He is responsible for its outcome:

> For unto us a Child is born, Unto us a Son is given; And the government will be upon His shoulder. And His name will be called Wonderful, Counselor, Mighty God, Everlasting Father, Prince of Peace (Isaiah 9:6).

This isn't just a poetic Christmas-time verse. It's our promise. Our Wonderful, Counselor, Mighty God, Everlasting Father, and Prince of Peace is responsible. He carries the burden of the outcome. Authority is on His shoulders. Enforcement is on His shoulders. Everything is on His shoulders. The only thing on our shoulders is to be good and faithful managers of what He has given us to manage in our lives, if we'll accept the task.

So what kind of managers are we? Are we prudent? Are we joyful? Are we happy? Are we successful? Are we useful? Are we devoted? Are we 100% consumed with what God's given us to manage? Are we all those things? A good and faithful steward has no burden of the outcome. Our only burden is to do what is asked of us, which I admit is a lot if you've been paying attention. Are we doing it? Even then, He amazingly enables us to do it. What a good deal we've got! "For My yoke is easy and My burden is light" (Matthew 11:30, NIV).

MANAGING EVERYWHERE

My son, Daniel, was in track when he was about seven or eight years old. So while he was in track, our family ran with him. His sister Charity ran a 5K with him. I ran a 5K with him. We all supported him. We prepared him. He ran two races with us.

God says He won't put on us more than we can bear. He prepares us. Sometimes we feel we can just run the race without stretching, or learning how to breathe while we run, and how to pace ourselves. Spiritually this would be studying to show ourselves approved, praying without ceasing, learning wisdom and maturity though hearing the voice of God, and obeying His Word. When we are not prepared, we can get a cramp, get short of breath, or we don't finish the race because we get too tired. Then the burden seems heavy, and that is when we feel it is more than we can bear. Many give up.

Well, the last 5K Daniel did, he decided he wanted to run on his own. Since he was only seven or eight, I was nervous. I mean, it's a 5K! But there were a lot of kids running, including his whole track team, so I let him run it without a family member alongside.

Near the finish line, Charity, other family members, and I were waiting for Daniel to finish along with the other kids' families. As kids were coming in, we're yelling, "Yeah! Yay! You did it!"as we cheered for all the kids. And they started uniting with their parents and being cheered on to the end. Then one parent left with his child. Another person left with her child. Then another.

And I'm thinking, "Where's my child?" We were usually in the middle of the pack when we ran 5Ks with Daniel, so I thought he was a pretty good runner. So I kept watching. People were leaving. It was getting dark. And I start thinking, "I'm a horrible parent. Why would I ever let him go by himself? Someone's grabbed him along the way; he's been kidnapped!" All you parents will know the thoughts that can come to a parent's mind.

All of a sudden I see a flashing light. It's a police car. And right in front of the police car, there's Daniel. As we saw him coming in, everyone who was still there came back over to the finish line to cheer for him: "Yeah! Come on! You can do it! Keep going, keep going!"

When Daniel got to the finish line, I grabbed him and asked, "Daniel, are you OK?" He replied, "I did great, Mom! I did so good! That car followed me the whole way flashing his lights! And did you see everybody come cheer for me?"

That's exactly what he said. So our whole family agreed: "Yes sir, Daniel, you were amazing! That was awesome!"

But Daniel did do great. He prepared and finished the race set before him—not in the "everyone-gets-a-participation-prize" way. He did great because he did what he was able to do. Even though it was funny, and we all still laugh about it today, I knew he did what he knew how to do.

> Therefore we also, since we are surrounded by
> so great a cloud of witnesses, let us lay aside

every weight, and the sin which so easily ensnares us, and let us run with endurance the race that is set before us" (Hebrews 12:1, NKJV).

Every area of our lives has something for us to manage. Details we don't want to drop. Things we need to do. Things to remember. Things to follow up on. Deadlines to meet. But it's not just the facts of what we accomplish that matter; it's how well we run our own race.

In this case, running our race well means managing ourselves well. We manage our thoughts, our bodies, our souls, our time, our families, our finances, and our work. As long as we have breath, we are managers. Whether it's a big goal or a little one, or whether we seem to be good at it or not, what matters is that we are good and faithful anyway. What matters to God is what we do with what He has given us to manage. It's all His. We're just managing.

PRAYER AND ACTIVATION

Make a list of all the areas you personally have to manage, then pray this prayer with me and ask God to show you at least one other area of management you didn't realize you had.

God, only You give responsibility. You're the One who asks more of me. You promise not to give me more than I can bear, so if You're asking me to rise into more responsibility, I trust You. I trust You that it's something I'm capable of, and I trust You to give me grace and wisdom to steward this responsibility well. Show me the areas You see as my responsibility and remind me daily that You are the owner. I'm just managing what You trust me to manage. In Jesus' name. Amen.

Endnotes:

[23]Messie2vie. οἰκονόμος - oikonómos [oy-kon-om'-os]. Retrieved from https://www.messie2vie.fr/bible/strongs/strong-greek-G3623-oikonomos.html.

[24]Zodhiates, Spiros, Hebrew-Greek Key Word Study Bible, AMG Publishers, Chattanooga, TN 37422, U.S.A., Copyright (C) 1984 by AMG International, Inc.

Chapter 6

STEWARDING OUR THOUGHTS

Have you ever watched a bird build a nest? Well, I haven't, except maybe on *National Geographic*™. But there's a saying my Dad likes to use: "A bird may land on your head, but that doesn't mean you have to let it build a nest and hatch its eggs there!"

This got me thinking about whether a bird could actually build a nest on a person's head. That's crazy! The bird would have to make the same trip to the person's head, over and over and over and over. Every time the bird came back, it would be carrying the same thing—one small twig. Over, and over, and over, and over. Who would sit around long enough to let that happen?

All of us. The thing is, that is exactly what happens with our thoughts! We let it happen more often than we'd like to think.

Let's look at a scenario. The Bible says if you hate someone, you've committed murder in your heart. Well, I'm pretty sure you wouldn't murder. And you probably try not to hate people either. If you feel hatred toward someone and you're a Christian, you may think, "Oh, that's bad. I have to choose to love him/her." Good for you! But just like murder wasn't your first reaction, neither was hatred. The hatred came later. So what came first?

Can you remember back to a time earlier in your life when you got really angry at someone? Maybe it was your spouse when you were newlyweds or a coworker when you first started your job. That first thought of anger probably wasn't that big. It certainly wasn't, "I want that person to die!" That would be crazy. It probably was something much smaller, such as, "Why would he do that? That's so inconsiderate!"

Thoughts that take root in our hearts and grow ungodly fruit are rarely all that shocking at first. They're more likely to be something that may not be good, but also isn't the end of the world. They're just a twig. If a bird dropped one twig on my head, I wouldn't like it, but it wouldn't be a life-altering moment either. The thought, "he's so inconsiderate" is just one small twig of thought. It might even be true! That one small twig is not a big deal by itself. But if you keep feeding the anger about how inconsiderate a person in your life is, you very well could find yourself with baby hatred hatching on your head.

Our thoughts are the source of every action we take. We might catch ourselves saying something we want to take back, and then say, "Oops! I don't know why I said that." Well, the reason we said it is that we first thought it. And in order for thoughts to come out of our mouths, we probably repeated them in our minds several times first.

WHO IS RESPONSIBLE?

When thoughts come to our mind that shouldn't, it doesn't matter so much where they came from. What matters most is what we do with them. We all have crazy thoughts. Lord help us if every thought we ever had was broadcast to the world! Life, work, people, and the enemy can all intrude on our thoughts, but it's up to us how we respond. Do we agree with the negative thought that our spouse or coworker is inconsiderate? Or do we recognize such thoughts are not God's best and choose to do something with those thoughts so they don't become part of us?

The first time an ungodly thought comes to us, sure, maybe it did come from an outside source. But once it crosses our mind, the power is ours to do whatever we will do with it. God has given us the power to not be ruled by our thoughts. We are to rule over our thoughts. How? By choosing them.

Being a good steward of our thoughts means causing our thoughts to be good, pleasing, and excellent, in the interest of others and subject to God's will. It's up to us to produce thoughts pleasing to God as good and faithful stewards of the minds He gave us. Our minds are not our own. Your mind is a gift from Him! So is my mind. But it is our responsibility to steward these gifts well by choosing to implant godly thoughts. That's right—God tells us what to think!

Since our thoughts affect literally everything about us and around us, this is a pretty big issue to learn to steward well. Proverbs 23:7 says, "As [someone] thinks within himself, so he is" (NASB). We have to learn to steward our thoughts in order to be good and faithful servants. We can do this by renewing our minds, praying without ceasing, capturing our thoughts, and looking for good thoughts. Let's see what the Manual says about each of these.

RENEW THE MIND

The first step to choosing godly thoughts is renewing our minds with the Word of God. Romans 12:2 says, "Do not be conformed to this world, but be transformed by the renewal of your mind" (ESV). Renewing the mind is transformative. Of course it is! Our minds are responsible for just about everything else we do. The best way to renew our minds is through the Word of God. "All Scripture is breathed out by God and profitable for teaching, for reproof, for correction, and for training in righteousness" (2 Timothy 3:16, ESV). The Bible will correct our thoughts. It will teach us what thoughts we should entertain and what thoughts we should throw away. It will even keep us from sin: "I have stored up your word in my heart, that I might not sin against you" (Psalm 119:11, ESV).

The Bible is not a one-and-done book. You don't read it and then check it off your list as something you accomplished. The Bible is alive. That means we can read the same verse every year of our lives, and it can have entirely new implications for us each year. It is alive like you and I are. As our needs change and our perspectives change, so will what we receive from a verse. The revelation contained in the Word of God is able to meet us at every stage of our lives and in every circumstance. This is what the Bible says about itself:

> For the Word of God is living and active, sharper than any two-edged sword, piercing to the division of soul and of spirit, of joints and of marrow, and discerning the thoughts and intentions of the heart (Hebrews 4:12, ESV).

Imagine that, the Bible even helps us discern our own thoughts and intents so we can keep renewing our minds and being transformed. It's a flashlight on whatever we need to see at this time to be transformed into the image of Christ (Psalm 119:105).

If we're lacking anything in our thought-lives, the first solution is the Word of God. If we have any confusion, any struggle, any doubt, or any need at all in our thought-lives, it is a need for the Word of God. We cannot get too much of it. How can we even get enough of it?

> Blessed is the man who walks not in the counsel of the wicked, nor stands in the way of sinners, nor sits in the seat of scoffers; but his delight is in the law of the Lord, and on his law he meditates day and night. He is like a tree planted by streams of water that yields its fruit

in its season, and its leaf does not wither. In all that he does, he prospers (Psalm 1:1-6, ESV).

That is the Bible. That is our Manual.

PRAY WITHOUT CEASING

If you have ever traveled with Dr. Bill Hamon, you may have noticed something funny. He is always praying in tongues. Riding in the back of Ubers® and Lyfts®, he prays in tongues. After a waiter or waitress takes his order and moves on to the next person at the table, he prays in tongues. Walking through the airport, he prays in tongues. And it's not even just during travel or "ministry" times. He prays in tongues at home and in the car and in the doctor's office. I would have thought it was impossible to "pray without ceasing," but my dad does it—and so can you! Wherever you are, it doesn't have to be out loud. We have all been talking to someone or doing something while our minds are also wandering elsewhere. In the same way, you can continually be praying in your mind.

The Manual tells us to use our thoughts specifically for praying and to do it all the time. I guess we have a lot less time to build bird's nests if we're busy praying!

CAPTURE THE BAD

Second Corinthians 10:5 says, "Casting down imaginations, and every high thing that exalteth itself against the knowledge of God, and bringing into captivity every thought to the obedience of Christ."

What? I have to take my own thoughts captive? I have to restrain them and make them obedient? But I'm a free spirit! Many of us have thought like this, but I have good news for you. The ability to capture our bad thoughts is freedom from God's point of view. It's a choice He places before us (Deuteronomy 30:19). When we choose to capture the bad, it brings us freedom. He wants us to take evil thoughts captive because He took darkness captive so that we can be free. We are to be like Him. As a good Father, He wants us to get rid of evil the way He would. Look at this Scripture in Genesis:

> And God saw that the wickedness of man was great in the earth, and that every imagination of the thoughts of his heart was only evil continually. And it repented the Lord that he had made man on the earth, and it grieved him at his heart (Genesis 6:5-6).

If we let evil thoughts roam freely and multiply, it grieves God. Taking them captive—just like He took darkness captive—pleases God.

LOOK FOR THE GOOD

Whatever we think on grows until it can eventually consume our lives; whatever we don't shrinks and eventually dies out. So if we want good, pleasing, excellent thoughts that are in the interest of others and subject to God's will, we should find the good ones we already have and think on them more:

Finally, brothers, whatever is true, whatever is
honorable, whatever is just, whatever is pure,
whatever is lovely, whatever is commendable, if
there is any excellence, if there is anything
worthy of praise, think about these things
(Philippians 4:8, ESV).

There is always something good to find. I have realized
no matter what happens to me in life someone always has
it worse than me, and he may even seem to be managing
it better than I am managing my situation. The key is
how we react to the situation which I believe starts with
how we think about it. We can think of ourselves either
as victims or as survivors. Dwelling on the negative will
bring us down which means we are not managing our
thoughts well. God is telling us to think on the positive in
our lives.

God works all things together for good. When you make
a cake, you add several ingredients: butter, flour, sugar,
milk, baking powder, salt, raw eggs, and flavoring. Flour,
salt, butter, raw eggs, and baking powder alone would
taste awful, but they are needed for the finished product.
We are like cake. Sometimes we are going through the
bad-tasting parts of our lives, but if we think, "This is just
one part in making me into the image of Christ (a good
cake)," then we can manage the situation better.

GET RID OF WORRY

There's a famous quote that is funny, but true: "My life
has been filled with worries of terrible misfortune, most
of which never happened."[25]

How many of the things we worry about never happen? A recent study says that it is 85 percent! So 85 percent of what we worry about never actually happens. Worry, fear, and anxiety fill our thoughts when we let them. Since 85 percent of it never happens, from a management perspective, that's a terrible use of resources!

In Isaiah 55:8 and 9, God says His thoughts are not our thoughts. His ways aren't our ways. So we don't even know what His thoughts are about whatever we are worried about, unless we take time to learn them. If we are weak in an area, He has thoughts and ways that will build us up. But we do know one thing for sure: worry is not His way.

> "Therefore I say to you, do not worry about your life, what you will eat or what you will drink; nor about your body, what you will put on. Is not life more than food and the body more than clothing? Look at the birds of the air, for they neither sow nor reap nor gather into barns; yet your heavenly Father feeds them. Are you not of more value than they? Which of you by worrying can add one cubit to his stature? So why do you worry about clothing? Consider the lilies of the field, how they grow: they neither toil nor spin; and yet I say to you that even Solomon in all his glory was not arrayed like one of these. Now if God so clothes the grass of the field, which today is, and tomorrow is thrown into the oven, will He not much more clothe you, O you of little faith? Therefore do not worry, saying, 'What

shall we eat?' or 'What shall we drink?' or 'What shall we wear?' For after all these things the Gentiles seek. For your heavenly Father knows that you need all these things. But seek first the kingdom of God and His righteousness, and all these things shall be added to you. Therefore do not worry about tomorrow, for tomorrow will worry about its own things. Sufficient for the day is its own trouble" (Matthew 6:25-34, NKJV).

Whatever you're worried about, you don't have to think about it. God's got you. These Scriptures in Matthew are Him saying:

> *I got you. Don't worry about it. I've got it taken care of. I've already done it. You don't have to think about it or worry about it. Instead, think on those things that are pure and lovely and of good report and just. Those are the things I want you to think about. Not worry!*

Worry will never produce good fruit in our lives. It's not being a good and faithful steward of the powerful brain God has given us. Worry is the power of believing in reverse.

Stephen Covey says this about our thoughts: "Sow a thought, reap an action. Sow an action, reap a habit. Sow a habit, reap a character. Sow a character, reap a destiny."[26] God, our Father, wants to give us every good and perfect gift. He just asks that we have His perspective, especially in the difficult things[27]—that we set our mind on things above.[28] It's His mind anyway; we're just managing it.

Today, take inventory of your thought life and whether it's producing the destiny you feel called to or that you desire.

PRAYER AND ACTIVATION

We each have our strengths and weaknesses when it comes to our thought lives. What is one type of thought that runs freely through your mind at times that doesn't line up with God's Word? For example, it may be that worrisome thoughts tend to fill your mind, or perhaps negative thoughts about yourself bombard you often, or maybe jealousy or envy prick at your heart when you're unsuspecting. Acknowledge which of these thoughts most oppose you, and then insert it in the blanks below as you pray this prayer with me:

Lord, I confess to You that thoughts of _____ often try to fill my mind. As Your Word says, I acknowledge these thoughts as not being from You and choose to take them captive to the obedience of Christ. The thought of _____ is not part of Your thoughts toward me. Thank You, Lord, that Your thoughts toward me are good—to give me a hope and a future. Thank You that You have given me the mind of Christ. Help me replace the thoughts of _____ with thoughts from Your Word and Your Spirit instead, so that I can steward well the mind You have given me. In Jesus' name. Amen.

Endnotes:

[25]"Michael de Montaigne > Quotes > Quotable Quotes," goodreads.com, accessed January 3, 2019, https://www.goodreads.com/quotes/489558-my-life-has-been-filled-with-terrible-misfortune-most-of.

[26]Covey, S. R. (2004). Seven Habits of Highly Effective People. London, U.K.: Simon and Schuster.

[27]James 1:17.

[28]Colossians 3.

Chapter 7

STEWARDING OUR BODIES

A lot of us put our faith out for something and then get discouraged when we don't see results. I have a collection of VHS and DVD workouts. I used to buy all the latest ones. Every new infomercial had me mesmerized thinking about the brand-new person I would be in just six weeks! I had everything from Jane Fonda's and Cindy Crawford's workouts to Pilates and yoga. I may even have a pair of leg warmers and a leotard in the back of my closet somewhere!

But no matter how many workout videos I bought or watched back in the day, I never developed a six pack or buns of steel. That's the problem with having faith without works. We put our faith and even our money out (buy the DVD), then get discouraged when we don't see results (look like Cindy Crawford). We may even go to church (watch the DVD), but if we are not Christ-like and obedient outside church (actually do the exercises), then we will not see the results, and neither will others. Then we start to think God's Word must not be true, just like the exercise infomercial that made all kinds of promises. God makes us promises, but we must not only hear them, but also be obedient to do His Word (James 2:20).

I have a lot of information about what I should do with my body. That doesn't mean I do it. That doesn't even mean I want to do it. I'm starting to know what Paul meant in Romans 7:19 when he said the things he wants to do, he doesn't do. He probably didn't have a muscular six-pack either. Wanting and doing are two different things. Tell me I'm not alone in this!

As Christians we used to think that the physical body was not that important in the grand scheme of things. We looked forward to dying so we could "fly away, oh glory." But just like God cares about our lives on earth, He cares about our bodies. They are His, not ours:

> Or do you not know that your body is the temple of the Holy Spirit who is in you, whom you have from God, and you are not your own? For you were bought at a price; therefore glorify God in your body and in your spirit, which are God's (1 Corinthians 6:19-20, NKJV).

Sure, our bodies may not be the most important thing about us, but they certainly are important to God. They are His temple! God's temple is extremely important to Him. He was so specific about how to build the Temple in the Old Testament. And He was picky about who was allowed in and how they were allowed to behave. He even got angry when His people cared more about their own houses than they did about His.[29]

THE NEW TEMPLE

God didn't change. In the Old Testament, the Temple was a natural building. But when Jesus ripped the veil and gave us all access to Him, He made a new home for Himself. We all love the idea that we have access to Him. He is in our hearts. He dwells in us. That's a major highlight of the new covenant we have. It's exciting! But, it also brings responsibility. We forget that our literal physical bodies are His literal physical temple. He gave up His majestic, ornate Temple made of the finest materials in the known world. He gave up the Ark of the Covenant. He gave up all that He dwelled in because He preferred to dwell in us.

Think of the prettiest building you know. That's what the Temple of God was like. It was gorgeous! At least it was supposed to be. And instead of living in that house, He wanted to live in us.

Now think of your own house. If the roof leaks, you fix it. If a light bulb blows out, you replace it. When the season changes, you probably redecorate it, not because it's critical to living but because it's fun and beautiful. You enjoy it more. Think how much you enjoy your house.

We are God's house. Do we make His house as enjoyable as we make our own?

"'Is it time for you yourselves to dwell in your paneled houses, and this temple to lie in ruins?' Now therefore, thus says the Lord of hosts: 'Consider your ways! You have sown much, and bring in little; You eat, but do not have enough; You drink, but you are not filled with drink; You clothe yourselves, but no one is warm; And he who earns wages, Earns wages to put into a bag with holes.' Thus says the Lord of hosts: 'Consider your ways!'" (Haggai 1:4-7, NKJV).

It's time to consider our ways. This isn't just an Old Testament idea either, but it isn't a popular concept today. You may be sitting there thinking, "Oh come on, there are some things that are mine. My body is definitely my own." If you ask any feminist who is pro-abortion, she'll tell you right away her body is her own. She can do what she will with it. Anyway, God wouldn't tell you what to do with your own body as long as it isn't affecting anyone else, right? It's your body. You're not hurting anyone. Well, let's see what God has to say in His Manual.

First Corinthians 3:16-17 says this:

Don't you know that you yourselves are God's temple and that God's Spirit dwells in your midst? If anyone destroys God's temple, God will destroy that person; for God's temple is sacred, and you together are that temple (NIV).

That's a pretty strong statement. God will destroy someone who destroys His temple. Yikes! I never want that to happen. I never want to destroy His temple. Sometimes we think that God was only "strong" with people like this in the Old Testament, that since Jesus came, we all get a free pass at our behavior as long as we confess our sins to Him. But this is a New Testament Scripture, and it's pretty strong to me.

We shouldn't really be too surprised by God's expectations about our bodies. This body of mine is His. Your body is His. Not only are our bodies His to live in, but they are also His to rent to us. It's not up to us to share our bodies with Him. They are His. He gave them to us as tenants. He really owns the property. This hand I'm typing with is not mine. It was bought with a price. He paid for it. "Therefore glorify God in your body and in your spirit, which are God's" (1 Corinthians 6:20, NKJV). So is it your body? No, sorry, not yours. It's going to go in the ground, and it's going to decay. You're just renting the space until then. "Know that the LORD is God. It is he who made us, and we are his" (Psalm 100:3, NIV).

SMOKING INDOORS AND OTHER POLICIES

Where I live there are laws about smoking indoors in public establishments. Every establishment is governed by those laws, including rental properties. For a while I helped manage a vacation rental property. Our policy was that guests had to smoke outside and couldn't smoke indoors. It's simple. Not everyone who's going to use that house is a smoker. So those who aren't smokers don't want to be exposed to the smoke from previous renters. Smoking wasn't the only thing we had rules about. In order to have a shared space, there had to be order. Things had to work for all the tenants.

If we're tenants of these bodies God owns and we're sharing space with Him, then He has rules to make it work. Galatians 6:8 says, "For he who sows to his flesh will of the flesh reap corruption, but he who sows to the Spirit will of the Spirit reap everlasting life" (NKJV).

Many people think, "So what if I smoke? If I smoke, I drink, I do drugs, I'm in sexual immorality, I'm a glutton, so what? I'm not hurting anybody but myself. If I'm anorexic or bulimic or I cut myself, or if I am just passive and don't do anything good for my body, so what? What's the big deal?" It's a very big deal! God is thinking, *"Hey I own this space. I have just given this space to you to manage. I'm the owner of this space. This is My temple, and if you're going to manage it, you better take care of it."*

If I had renters in the vacation house, and they didn't take care of it by following the policies, there were consequences. It was in their best interest to follow the policies. If they brought in poison, destroyed things, had guests stay who weren't authorized or accounted for, hoarded a bunch of stuff, left stains or holes in the walls, brought pets without permission, or any other behavior that wasn't in the book, it cost them. It's not that I wanted to punish them, but their behavior had consequences. Sometimes I learned to put new things in the policy manual after finding out what people might do that is destructive. But if it was destructive, just because it wasn't clearly spelled out in the policy manual doesn't mean I didn't enforce consequences. They also had to take into consideration the nature of the policies, which basically could be summed up: don't cause damage.

It might even be a sacrifice to do the right thing with our bodies:

> Therefore, I urge you, brothers and sisters, in view of God's mercy, to offer your bodies as a living sacrifice, holy and pleasing to God—this is your true and proper worship. Do not conform to the pattern of this world, but be transformed by the renewing of your mind. Then you will be able to test and approve what God's will is—his good, pleasing and perfect will (Romans 12:1-2, NIV).

Our bodies are a living sacrifice. That means the sacrifice it takes each of us to care for the body God has given us is appropriate. It's our worship. It's worth it. What kinds of things are a sacrifice?

- Eating and drinking in a way that glorifies God. "So whether you eat or drink or whatever you do, do it all for the glory of God" (1 Corinthians 10:31, NIV).
- Keeping our bodies trained and active: "For physical training is of some value..." (1 Timothy 4:8, NIV).
- Taking the proper medicine when we need it: "No longer drink only water, but use a little wine for your stomach's sake and your frequent infirmities" (1 Timothy 5:23, NKJV). (Drinking water was often unsanitary and caused stomach problems.

Paul was prescribing a solution for that day.)
- Not overindulging. "It is not good to eat much honey, nor is it glorious to seek one's own glory." (Proverbs 25:27, ESV).
- Staying sober: "And do not be drunk with wine, in which is dissipation; but be filled with the Spirit" (Ephesians 5:18, NKJV).
- Staying sexually pure: "Now the body is not for sexual immorality but for the Lord, and the Lord for the body" (1 Corinthians 6:13, NKJV).

Now the works of the flesh are evident, which are: adultery, fornication, uncleanness, lewdness…and the like; of which I tell you beforehand, just as I also told you in time past, that those who practice such things will not inherit the kingdom of God (Galatians 5:19-21, NKJV).

None of these is actually that difficult, but it can feel like it sometimes. Saying "no" to an extra spoonful of Grannie Barbara's homemade banana pudding certainly feels sacrificial! Today we have more temptations not to make the right choice than ever before.

God is renting His body out to each of us. He has a Manual about what to do with the body. Even if something isn't spelled out in the Manual, one thing is clear: take good care of it. Keep it clean. Keep it presentable. Keep it honorable. So what kind of renters are we? What kind of managers are we of God's house, our bodies? Are we good renters? Are we bad renters? Are we good managers? All of the fitness infomercials I used to watch about taking care of my body amount to nothing more than a collection of DVDs if I don't actually take care of my body. Remember doing, not just knowing, is part of being a good and faithful steward.

God owns our bodies so much that we can't even heal them ourselves. He has given us wisdom and knowledge through doctors and modern science, but even that is limited. It's His body. He formed it. Only He can heal it. But the awesome thing is that He will heal it. Even if we have poorly managed parts of our bodies, or even if we feel like we could have done better, God has grace. He wants us to have long life and be in health. He promises to do those things for us. All He wants is for us to have His heart and nature—to be conformed to His image. It's His body anyway. We're just managers.

ACTIVATION

It's time to consider our ways just like God told the Israelites. Let's do it now. I'll do it with you. Let's answer these questions:

- Do I take care of broken things in my house more quickly than I take care of issues in my body?
- Do I prevent damage in my home more effectively than I prevent damage to my body?
- Do I clean and make my home presentable more than I do my body?
- Am I more likely to invest money on my home than I am on my body?

- Do I justify treating my body poorly by saying I'm not hurting anyone else?
- Do I do things to my body that defile it with sin?

If you recognize a way that you have not been a good steward of your body, ask God to forgive you now. His mercies are new every morning, but you don't even have to wait until morning to begin stewarding your body well!

Endnotes:
[29]Exodus 26; 1 Chronicles 28; 1 Kings 6; Haggai 1:2-10.

Chapter 8

STEWARDING OUR TIME

When I was in high school, I was very social. I had always struggled in school because I was dyslexic and didn't realize it until my sophomore year, so my priority was my friends, drill team, and having fun. I wasn't wise with my time. My brothers, on the other hand, made academics their priority, and they made straight "A's." They were wise with their time. They still had friends and were in the band and football. I did OK, but because it was always such a struggle, I just learned to get by.

We all do that in some areas of our lives. We don't want to put the time and sacrifice into something we feel inferior in or that doesn't come as easy to us. What is important to us is what we will make time for. Making an "A" on a test was not that important to me, so I didn't take the time to study. I was fine with just passing the test so I could move on to the next level with my friends and not get in trouble with my parents. That's what I wanted to do with my time.

What do you do with your time? Really think about your time and what you do with it. Maybe you go to work. You go to church. You spend time with friends and important relationships. You take care of your home and your children. You take care of yourself—eating, grooming, and sleeping. These are all good things to do and should be done.

Now think about this. The time it takes to do those things is God's time. Our time is not ours. It's not ours because everything belongs to Him. We are not only on God's time at church; we are always on God's time. What have we been doing with His time? We know what it's like to be on someone else's time. Every job we've had was not our time, but someone else's. We couldn't do whatever we wanted during that time. We couldn't sit back and watch a movie at work. We couldn't leave and go shopping while on the clock.

We're always on God's time. He paid for our time. We don't get to choose what we do with our time. The only choice we have is whether we will choose to serve Him: "And if it seems evil to you to serve the Lord, choose for yourselves this day whom you will serve...But as for me and my house, we will serve the Lord" (Joshua 24:15, NKJV).

I believe you and I want the same thing: to serve Him— to choose His time—to be good stewards of the time He delegates to us. That's why you're reading this book, and that's why I'm writing it. I want to hear, "Well done, good and faithful servant; you were a wise steward of your time" in regard to the time I have here on the earth. But time isn't just a running clock. God has seasons and paces that affect our time. To steward time well, we've got to know His view of it.

UNDERSTANDING THE SEASON— REDEEMING THE TIME

My mom wrote a little book, *The Spiritual Seasons of Life* (Christian International), in which she shows how God brings seasons in our lives just like nature has seasons. If you don't know the season, you could get pretty frustrated. You could be putting effort entirely in the wrong place. If it's winter and everything has gone dormant, but you expect it to be summer and harvest time, you'll be pretty discouraged about where you are. And you'll feel like you're failing if you try to harvest in the dead of winter.

It helps to know the seasons if we're going to make the most of the time God has given us. Proverbs 29:18 says, "If people can't see what God is doing, they stumble all over themselves; But when they attend to what he reveals, they are most blessed" (MSG). That's us! We can be most blessed by seeing what season God has us in.

God has something for us to do with every season of our time. There is a season for everything:

> A time to be born and a time to die,
> a time to plant and a time to uproot,
> a time to kill and a time to heal,
> a time to tear down and a time to build,
> a time to weep and a time to laugh,

a time to mourn and a time to dance,
a time to scatter stones and a time to gather them,
a time to embrace and a time to refrain from
   embracing,
a time to search and a time to give up,
a time to keep and a time to throw away,
a time to tear and a time to mend,
a time to be silent and a time to speak,
a time to love and a time to hate,
a time for war and a time for peace"
(Ecclesiastes 3:2-8, NIV).

I think the above just about covers it. God has His times and seasons for everything in our lives. We just need to hear God's voice to know what season it is.

Some seasons are obvious. When a loved one dies, that is a time to weep and mourn. We really don't have much control over our time to be born or die, but for many occasions and decisions in our lives, we need to know God's timing, and it is not always clear. We need the Word (is it in God's Word?), the Will (is it God's will?), and the Way (God's timing and how) of God. Many times we get discouraged because we only have 2 or even 1 out of the 3. We know it is in God's Word; we know it's God's will, but it's the wrong time. Maybe the time is right, and we know it is in God's Word, but that is not God's will for you. "In the mouth of two or three witnesses shall every word be established" (2 Corinthians 13:1). These are ways to get confirmation on a decision you are about to make.

"Be very careful, then, how you live—not as unwise but as wise, making the most of every opportunity, because the days are evil. Therefore do not be foolish, but understand what the Lord's will is" (Ephesians 5:15-17, NIV). So watch your step. Use your head. Make the most of every chance you get. These are desperate times! Here's what it says in another translation: "Don't live carelessly, unthinkingly. Make sure you understand what the Master wants" (v. 17, MSG).

"Be wise in the way you act toward outsiders; make the most of every opportunity" (Colossians 4:5, NIV). Make the most of every opportunity. Make the most of every chance you get. You cannot undo one second of your life. You cannot relive one second of your life. So be wise with your time.

We must live in God's times and seasons. We can't be in a rush to go to the next thing. Just do well now—managing today's time according to what He has for us.

CONSTANT IN EVERY SEASON

In every season, there are some specific things we are to keep doing. These things aren't seasonal. They're not optional if we're going to follow the Manual. They're required. Let's look at what things are consistent in every season.

Unto the Glory of God
No matter what we do, it is to be unto the glory of God. There's an easy test that may show us if we did something to the glory of God. If we hear ourselves say, "I earned that," then maybe we think we did it unto our own glory. Maybe we think our time was ours, and since we spent "our" time on it, we somehow earned it. But if our time

81

belongs to God, we earned nothing. It's all His! We might want to say, "I earned that. I put a lot of time into that." The question is did we put the time in so we would get credit for it? Or did we do it as unto the glory of God?

"And whatsoever ye do, do it heartily, as to
the Lord, and not unto men"
(Colossians 3:23).

Not doing it unto men includes not doing it unto ourselves. That task on our to-do list? It only matters in as much as it is unto the Lord. That New Year's resolution? It also belongs to the Lord. That deadline you have to meet? God owns it.

Children get in trouble sometimes because of peer pressure, and honestly adults do too. It is normal to want to please others, and there is nothing wrong with that as long as it doesn't go against God's Word or what God has told you for your life. There is nothing wrong with eating unless God has called you to fast from food for a certain time. Maybe you are in a time of fasting and your friends or family say, "Let's all go out to eat." You say no, but then they talk you in to going, and you think, "I will just watch them eat." But then they say, "Just try this one bite. It is delicious!" Just one bite won't hurt; you think? Before you know it, you have broken the fast God had called you to do by trying to please man instead of the Lord.

We bring glory to God when we do what He has given us to do: "I glorified you on earth, having accomplished the work that you gave me to do" (John 17:4, ESV). That's pretty straightforward. If everything we do is what God gave us to do, and we do it unto the glory of God, then it's not our time. It's His time, His glory, His accomplishment.

Pray Without Ceasing

God says to pray without ceasing (1 Thessalonians 5:17). We talked about this in Chapter 6—"Stewarding Our Thoughts." Let me just mention two more things about it. "Pray without ceasing" doesn't mean we need to stay in our prayer closets praying from morning until night. That would not be the best use of our time. (Unless it happens to be exactly what God asked us to do, in which case it would only be for a season). Instead, we can be in an attitude of prayer consistently. We can keep reminding ourselves to pray. Evangelist Smith Wigglesworth never went more than thirty minutes without praying. Prayer is something we're always supposed to do within the context of the time and season we're in.

The second thing is our time should also be spent praying for others in intercession. "Confess your faults one to another, and pray one for another, that ye may be healed. The effectual fervent prayer of a righteous man availeth much" (James 5:16). Jesus told His disciples to pray that God would send laborers. Jesus wanted laborers, and certainly God does too. So, why did Jesus say pray for them to come? Because God wants us to partner with Him in prayer for His will. One of the best ways I know to do this is to pray in tongues. By giving our time to praying even when we could be doing something else, we're honoring God and serving His purpose as well as serving others.

Assemble Ourselves Together

Hebrews 10:25 says, "Not forsaking the assembling of ourselves together, as is the manner of some, but exhorting one another, and so much the more as you see the Day approaching" (NKJV). You mean He's telling me I gotta go to church? Yep!

We are always supposed to assemble together, which means going to church. We will know God's will for our lives by studying His Word together and being equipped by the five-fold ministries. "Without counsel purposes are disappointed: but in the multitude of counsellors they are established" (Proverbs 15:22). We need oversight and counsel to help us know what God's will is in decisions we make and to help us navigate through life.

Some people think that they don't have time to go to church. They would have to give up something else to make the time, and it's something they don't want to sacrifice. Or if they work in ministry of some kind, they might think they already live a "church life," so going to their weekly assembly is unnecessary. But the Bible says otherwise. First, it says we have to make sacrifices to honor God, which includes sacrificing something we would rather do. And second, it says do not forsake assembling yourselves together, and it says this to people who were assembling as often as daily! Our culture of meeting an average of twice a week is not too frequent to say this Scripture does not apply. Assembling together with leaders and other believers is critical to stewarding our lives well.

Worship God

Worship leaders will like this one: we gotta worship.

> Praise ye the LORD. Praise the LORD, O my
> soul. While I live will I praise the LORD: I
> will sing praises unto my God while I have any
> being. Put not your trust in princes, nor in the
> son of man, in whom there is no help (Psalm
> 146:1-3).

Worship is part of all our seasons of life.[30] This means two things: we always have an attitude of worship, and we actively participate in a formal worship service. We do what the worship leader says. Raise our hands. Shout. Run. Dance. Whatever the worship leader is leading, we do because we're under authority. We know the authority we're under. When we enter our church and worship is happening, we are under the authority of the worship leader. So when the worship team is leading, we're going to do what they do. Yes, it is our personal worship to God, but it is also our response as a corporate Body under the authority of the Head—pleasing God in our unity.

Study to Show Ourselves Approved

We are to spend our time studying his Word to show ourselves approved (2 Timothy 2:15). We are to know God's Word (the Bible). When you are in school, you have to know the material to pass the test to go to the next grade level. If we don't know God's Word, we cannot pass the tests we face in our lives. We will never graduate to the next level in our walk with God.

Bring in the Harvest

Romans 13:11 says, "Besides this you know the time, that the hour has come for you to wake from sleep. For salvation is nearer to us now than when we first believed" (ESV). It's time for harvest. Jesus said there are not enough harvesters. The Bible teaches us about ways to harvest. It says help the poor. Help the widows. Go find someone—the elderly, the orphans, or the sick—and minister to them. Bring them in. The harvest is ripe. Harvesting is not just for evangelists. Actually, the evangelist's job is to equip all the saints to bring in the harvest (Ephesians 4:11). We are the saints; we are the harvesters. No matter what we are doing, we can bring the harvest by reaching out to those around us. This is not just witnessing on the streets, in church, or in a rally. This is day in and day out—at home, at work—in private and in public witnessing by how we live our lives. "Let your light so shine before men, that they may see your good works, and glorify your Father which is in heaven" (Matthew 5:16).

We all have a limited time on earth. What are we going to make our priority during the limited time we have? We have to be wise stewards of the time that God has given us. Time is our divine opportunity. It is God-given, so He has a purpose for it. All of our seasons, appointments, opportunities, and corresponding responsibilities have purpose. When we understand God's view of any given time, we can steward it well—good and faithfully. We want to study, worship, pray, bring in the harvest, assemble ourselves together, and give glory to God so we can get an "A" in the way we managed and prioritized our time. It's His time anyway. We're just managers.

ACTIVATION

Think of something you know God is going to help you accomplish. Maybe it's repairing a relationship with a family member. Maybe it's finding someone to mentor. Maybe it's getting married, getting out of debt, or earning a promotion. For me, it was writing this book.

Prayerfully consider a completion date for this accomplishment. It could be six weeks from now or two years. The timeline is up to you and God.

Now, think of three things you will need to do first to reach that goal. Here are some examples:

- To mentor someone, you probably need to decide who it's going to be, and then reach out to schedule meetings, and you may even want to do some studying about how mentor relationships work.
- To get out of debt, you may need to cancel some recurring unnecessary expenses, pick up a few extra hours or a side job, or sell some valuable items you're not attached to.

When you've thought of three things you can do to reach that goal, back up from your completion date and decide when you'll need to complete each of these three things. Then write them in your calendar! Being a good steward means being realistic. We aren't just waiting on God to fulfill what He promised. We have a part to play, and He will work with us to fulfill it.

Endnotes:
[30]Psalm 86:9; 95:6; 96:9; 99:5,9; 149:3; 134:2.

Chapter 9

GOOD AND FAITHFUL
WITH OUR FAMILIES

We all come from a family. We didn't get a choice about it. We could not choose to be born into the royal family or to be born into a poor family. We all just arrived. God is the One who decided what families we would be born into. It's all according to God's purpose for our lives. We could have been born into the strangest situation or into a more typical family setting, but either way we come from a family and God values that. God has called us to love and serve family as good stewards.

The subject of family covers a lot. There's a natural family: mom, dad, children, and spouses. Then there's the family of God—brothers and sisters in Christ.

We are called to be good stewards of our family. God expects us to serve our family, and He tells us how to do it in the Manual. We're actually not just serving them for their sakes to make them better. We serve them to build the character of God in us. We serve them because we're doing it unto Him. Serving our families, being good stewards of our families, is really serving God.

MOTHER AND FATHER—
THE AUTHORITY LEVEL

Our first exposure to family is to our mother and father. They are the people that conceived us. When they conceived us, they affected us. We got our genes from them. We might have heard their voices or sensed things they were experiencing. "Before I formed you in the womb, I knew you" (Jeremiah 1:5, NIV). At conception, we were impacted by our parents. Then either they or some parental figure with similar authority raised us.

Our first responsibility to family is to our parents according to Ephesians 6:2 which says, "Honor thy father and mother; which is the first commandment with promise—that it may be well with thee and thou mayest live long on the earth." This is the first commandment. God says that we must honor them. Honoring them does not mean that they do everything right or they are perfect. Honoring them means giving them the right value as our parents.

Our parents are our first natural authority figures, so maybe that's why honoring them is our first commandment. We learn how to obey through the authorities who raise us. They are meant to teach us discipline and consequences, how to listen and obey, and how to relate with our leaders for the rest of our lives. Our ability to honor our parents can affect our ability to honor God since He is our Heavenly Father. No matter how old we are, we are good stewards of our parental relationships when we honor them.

BROTHERS, SISTERS, SPOUSES— THE PEER LEVEL

Our next encounter with family is at a peer level. These are usually siblings (or maybe cousins or even friends). These are our "across" relationships. Later in life, members of the family of God often fill the sibling roles in our lives. On some level, all those we interact with function as peers, at least briefly. We're called to serve all these relationships, as we'll see in Chapter 12. We're to love our neighbor as ourselves (Luke 10:27). That pretty much means everyone!

For many, the most significant peer relationship we will be challenged to steward well is with our spouses. Let's look at what the Manual says about marriage:

"Husbands, love your wives, just as Christ loved the church and gave himself up for her" (Ephesians 5:25, NIV).

"In this same way, husbands ought to love their wives as their own bodies. He who loves his wife loves himself" (Ephesians 5:28, NIV).

"Husbands, love your wives and do not be harsh with them" (Colossians 3:19, NIV).

"Husbands, in the same way be considerate as you live with your wives, and treat them with respect as the weaker partner and as heirs with you of the gracious gift of life, so that nothing will hinder your prayers" (1 Peter 3:7, NIV).

"Wives, submit to your own husbands, as to the Lord" (Ephesians 5:22, ESV).

"Wives, likewise, be submissive to your own husbands, that even if some do not obey the word, they, without a word, may be won by the conduct of their wives" (1 Peter 3:1, NKJV).

"You shall not commit adultery" (Deuteronomy 5:18, NIV).

I think God put these verses in the Bible so that husbands and wives each would have Scriptures to argue with. "If you loved me like Christ loved the church, I wouldn't have any problem submitting to you…" "Well, if you submitted to me like the Bible said, then I wouldn't have any problem loving you like Christ loves the church." You know the argument, right? Of course I'm kidding! I actually believe God gave us balance so that neither spouse has the right to take advantage of the other. Both spouses must serve each other the way God intended in order to be good stewards of their marriage.

CHILDREN—THOSE WE RAISE UP

Finally, our last family encounter is with those we raise up: our children. We steward our kids by training them up the way the Manual tells us to. God's Word instructs us to "train up a child in the way he or (she) should go." We have to train our children. We train them to brush their teeth so that their teeth don't fall out when they get older. We train them to dress. We train them to bathe. We teach them to read, do math, and write. We educate them in natural things. We are being good stewards/parents when we train our children in natural and spiritual things.

When I was little my parents would take my brothers and me to church every Sunday. We not only went to church, we participated in church. One Sunday during praise and worship, everyone had their hands raised. That day I did not want to raise my hands so I kept them at my sides. My mom noticed and leaned down and whispered, "Raise your hands and praise the Lord." Well, I have a little bit of a stubborn streak and did not obey. So she told me again, "Raise your hands and praise the Lord." That time when I did not obey, she pinched on the lower part of my inner arm, twisting it a little for emphasis. As soon as she did that, the tears started flowing, my arms went up, and my hands went up. I was crying. After service people came up to Mom and said, "I was so blessed by your daughter and how the anointing had her crying with her hands lifted high."

You see, I was under authority and Mom made sure I knew who was the boss. She was training me up in the way I should go. Correction is a part of this process. Hebrews 12:6 says, "Because the Lord disciplines the one he loves, and he chastens everyone he accepts as his son" (NIV). God gives us the promise that if we train our children they will not depart from it. Learning to honor my mother and father, and family, was a part of this process. And later, learning to submit to my husband was also a part of the process.

We have to teach our children to behave, and then enforce it. Make them do it. I've heard parents say, "Well, I'm not going to tell my children that they have to worship because they may not want to praise the Lord when they get older." Well, then don't tell them to brush their teeth because they may not want to when they get older. Let those teeth fall right out. Don't tell them to get dressed, let them go to school naked because you don't want them to reject clothing and become a nudist when they grow up. "But worship, that's their choice. They'll have to make that choice when they're older." No. That's God's command. If a child doesn't learn to obey God's commands as a child, how will he or she do it as an adult? If we don't train them according to the Bible, we are not being good stewards/parents of their lives. It is our responsibility to train them spiritually as much as naturally. We as good stewards must educate them about the Word of God and serving Him. Most of us dedicate our children to the Lord when they are babies. We are saying, "They are Yours, Lord, and we give them to You; we will raise them according to Your Word."

God called Abraham to lay down his son's life, but spared him with a ram at the last minute. Abraham was a good steward with the son God gave him by being willing to do as God told him to do with his son. Being good stewards of our children means parenting by the Manual. Here are a few things the Bible says about raising kids:

"Fathers, do not exasperate your children; instead, bring them up in the training and instruction of the Lord" (Ephesians 6:4, NIV).

"Foolishness is bound in the heart of a child; but the rod
of correction shall drive it far from him"
(Proverbs 22:15).

"Withhold not correction from the child: for if thou
beatest him with the rod, he shall not die. Thou shalt
beat him with the rod, and shalt deliver his soul from
hell" (Proverbs 23:13).

"Train up a child in the way he should go: and when he is
old he will not depart from it" (Proverbs 22:6).

"But if anyone does not provide for his relatives, and
especially for members of his household, he has denied
the faith and is worse than an unbeliever"
(1 Timothy 5:8, ESV).

"In the fear of the Lord one has strong confidence, and
his children will have a refuge" (Proverbs 14:26, ESV).

Abraham's prophetic promises were changed to a sworn
oath by God Himself because he was willing to give God
his only son, Isaac, on the altar of sacrifice:

> Now I know that you fear God, since you have
> not withheld your son, your only son, from
> Me...By myself I have sworn, says the Lord,
> because you have done this thing, and have not
> withheld your son, your only son (Genesis
> 22:12, 16, NKJV).

My parents raised me by these Scriptures, and that's how
I raised my kids. When they were little, they were in

church with their hands raised. They were worshiping God, and they were praising the Lord. They didn't have a choice because they belong to God. God gave them to me to steward, so of course, it was for everyone's best that I stewarded the way the Manual says.

Another part of being good stewards of our kids is letting them see us obey God. Even when it means sacrificing. Mark 10:29 says, "There is no man that hath left house, or brethren, or sisters, or father, or mother, or wife, or children, or lands, for my sake, and the gospel's..." I believe family comes first, but to obey God, sometimes I had to leave my kids with a sitter so I could do what God was asking me to do. My dad traveled when I was young. All of our family has traveled when our kids were young and had to leave them sometimes. But you know what it says you're gonna get? "But he shall receive an hundredfold now in this time, houses, and brethren, and sisters, and mothers, and children, and lands, with persecutions; and in the world to come eternal life" (Mark 10:30). When we obey God, even if it costs our families in the short-term, we have been good stewards and will receive God's reward.

So what is there to do? Remember our families are not ours. Our parents are not ours. If they aren't perfect, or even if they are, they're God's. Our spouse is God's; God is responsible for him or her. Our kids are God's. They're just put in our care until they grow and become accountable to God for themselves. All our relationships belong to God. All we have to do is conduct ourselves the way God tells us in His Manual. He will do the rest! Then we can hear, "Well done, good and faithful servant." It's all His anyway. We're just managers.

ACTIVATION

Make a list of the family God has given you. You can make the list as extensive or brief as you want, including as few as just immediate family or as many as every relative you have. Some may be in authority in your life, some may be peers, and some may be ones you're raising up. Ask God to show you one thing to pray for each family member, and write it next to their names.

Pray now for your family, and keep your list somewhere you can look back over it later. I can't think of a simpler way to serve your family than to pray for them. It's free, fast, and you can do it in any situation. You'll be excited to one day look back and see the answer to the prayers you prayed for them.

Chapter 10

GOOD AND FAITHFUL
WITH OUR MONEY

Imagine a scenario with me. Imagine a man who is an alcoholic and drug addict. He's homeless and currently living in a box right out on the corner of your street. One day as you're leaving home, God speaks to you and tells you to give him $10,000. You know the man is intoxicated, and you can even see track marks on his arms. He is clearly an addict. Yet as you walk by, God says, "Give him $10,000." This is $10,000! What a large amount of money! You worked hard for it. It represents your life. This man will clearly use it for something bad, maybe even destroy himself with it. What do you do?

If you are obedient to God, you give the man $10,000. And of course, you are obedient to God! So you give him the money. Now what? Do you stand there to see if he is going to buy alcohol or drugs? Maybe he will, but is that what God said for you to do? Did God ask you to sit there and watch to see what he does with it? Were you a good manager? A good steward? Did you do your part?

Were you faithful? Were you wise? Yes! Because if God told you to do it, then that is all you need to know. God doesn't always tell us what is happening behind the scenes. The man may have been a minister who had lost his way, who will use the money to turn his life around and then lead many souls to Christ. He may have been someone who had just prayed, "God, give me $10,000 (thinking that would never actually happen), and I will serve you the rest of my life," who then changes his life and leads many souls to Christ. It isn't for us to judge. We are just to be obedient. Money is just a tool God gives us to use.

Being good and faithful servants with our money means accepting the truth. The truth is that it is not our money; it's God's. Everything is God's.

> Yours, Lord, is the greatness and the power and the glory and the majesty and the splendor, for everything in heaven and earth is yours. Yours, Lord, is the kingdom; you are exalted as head over all (1 Chronicles 29:11, NIV).

We are just called to manage what God has given us. We can't take it with us when we die. "For we brought nothing into this world, and it is certain we can carry nothing out" (1 Timothy 6:7). If we know it is His and not ours, it's so much easier to do what He says.

Most of us wouldn't even believe God was telling us to give $10,000 to a drug addict. But the $10,000 is His, and we trust Him. In order to be good stewards, we have to believe what God says about money. We have to believe both what the Bible says, as well as what He leads us to do by His Spirit. Believe it, and then practice it.

FAITH AND DEEDS

I told you in Chapter 7 about all the workout DVDs I own and have even watched, but don't really like to do. In the same way, we might go to a church that receives tithes and offerings. We might hear messages on what the Bible says about giving or about being wise with our money. But seeing, hearing, and learning God's principles about money won't cause His promises about money to come to pass any more than watching workout DVDs will tone our muscles. So we get discouraged because we give, and we don't see immediate results. Seeing and hearing are the first steps of faith, but the next step is action. Are we cheerful givers? Are we paying our tithes and offerings?

You know that famous Scripture that faith without works is dead? I can't help but notice what James was talking about when He said that. He was talking about meeting the physical needs of the poor with our resources.

> What good is it, my brothers and sisters, if someone claims to have faith but has no deeds? Can such faith save them? Suppose a brother or a sister is without clothes and daily food. If one of you says to them, "Go in peace; keep warm and well fed," but does nothing about their physical needs, what good is it? In the same way, faith by itself, if it is not accompanied by action, is dead (James 2:14-17, NIV).

This example is talking about our possessions. That includes money. The principle is true for everything. Believing without acting is death. There's probably a lot you believe about God's principles for money. How much of it are you doing? Some of these include tithing, sowing, not squandering, giving to the poor, and doing our part.

TITHING

Tithes and offerings are treated in the same way as everything else: a simple act of obedience. "Bring all the tithes into the storehouse" (Malachi 3:10, NKJV). Simple enough. Now we just have to do it. It's not our money. We are just a steward of what God has given us to cause it to produce the way He would have it produce.

It's also not our place to monitor where the tithes and offerings are spent in the church. Once it is given, it is in the stewardship of that ministry or church. So it leaves our stewardship and goes on to theirs. Now they are responsible to God for how they steward. It does not matter to us if they use it to pay the electric bill, buy new chairs, pay for the cleaning, or air conditioning. What matters is that we were obedient to do our part that God commanded us. "Will a man rob God? Yet you have robbed Me! But you say, 'In what way have we robbed You?' In tithes and offerings" (Malachi 3:8, NKJV). Yikes! Let's not make an excuse to rob God!

God wants us to do our part because it's best for us. He's not asking us to police everyone else. He's the boss. In fact He kind of just says, *"If you don't like it, suck it up and deal.*" Right? That's what it comes down to because if we don't like it, and we don't do it, we'll be cursed. But "If you are willing and obedient, you shall eat the good of the land" (Isaiah 1:19, ESV). Let's be willing and obedient!

ARGUMENTS AGAINST TITHING

Some people debate tithing. They say things like, "It's from the Old Covenant, not the New Covenant." Rather than continue the debate, let me just say this. When debating tithing at all, you forget one important principle. It's the principle of being under authority. We are called to submit to natural authority. If we're obeying God, then we attend the church God wants us planted in. If we attend the church God wants us planted in, then we obey the delegated authority God put over us, which is the leadership of that church. If the pastor and the church have an expectation of tithing, then even if we think the Bible frees us from that expectation, we must submit to the authority God put in our lives. If the leadership is wrong, he or she will account to God about it. But if we rebel against our church leaders, we are the ones who will be out from under God's delegated authority.

SOWING AND GIVING TO THE POOR

My dad is one of the biggest givers I've ever seen. I manage his books, and I'm constantly amazed at how generous above the tithe he is. But the thing is that he chooses to—and fights to—be that way, and he chooses to be happy and generous in all his giving. "So let each one give as he purposes in his heart, not grudgingly or of necessity; for God loves a cheerful giver" (2 Corinthians 9:7, NKJV).

That's the attitude God wants us to have about giving tithes and offerings.

Sometimes we sow because we believe in a vision: a ministry to help abused children, a disaster relief program, or a community center. Sometimes we sow because we're desperate for God to do something we know our money can't do. For example, we sow a seed toward a home we hope to one day own or toward being able to pay off debt. Sometimes we sow because God told us to even when we don't have a specific vision or faith for something. Whatever the reason, sowing is an important part of our faith in God. And all these scenarios have at least one thing in common: "But this I say: He who sows sparingly will also reap sparingly, and he who sows bountifully will also reap bountifully" (2 Corinthians 9:6, NKJV). To be good stewards, our sowing should be extravagant.

Extravagant means something different for everyone. You remember the widow's offering:

> Jesus sat down opposite the place where the offerings were put and watched the crowd putting their money into the temple treasury. Many rich people threw in large amounts. But a poor widow came and put in two very small copper coins, worth only a few cents. Calling his disciples to him, Jesus said, "Truly I tell you, this poor widow has put more into the treasury than all the others. They all gave out of their wealth; but she, out of her poverty, put in everything—all she had to live on" (Mark 12:41-44, NIV).

Jesus saw what the widow gave in the offering and what the rich man gave. Can you imagine if the pastor sat next to the offering plate and watched what you gave and then commented on how much you put in the offering? Most people would be very offended! But that is what Jesus did.

It doesn't matter how much you give or what you give as long as you are obedient and faithful to give from your heart whatever God is telling you. God looks at the heart and the motive behind all that you do. God will bless you if you are giving with the right attitude and motive.

Giving to those in need is part of our sowing. We can't possibly give to every need, but we can do our part to ease the burden of someone suffering:

"Do not withhold good from those to whom it is due, when it is in the power of your hand to do so" (Proverbs 3:27, NKJV).

"Share with the Lord's people who are in need. Practice hospitality" (Romans 12:13, NIV).

"The generous will themselves be blessed, for they share their food with the poor" (Proverbs 22:9, NIV).

"He who has pity on the poor lends to the Lord, and He will pay back what he has given" (Proverbs 19:17, NKJV).

Sowing and giving bring joy to God who loves a cheerful giver. They also bring joy and prosperity in our lives when we do with our money what God says to do with it.

SQUANDERING—THE PRODIGAL SPENDER

A look at our finances could tell us a lot about where we are faithful. What we spend shows our passion; it shows our beliefs. And when we use our finances to be faithful to God, we will be blessed. Proverbs says it like this: "A faithful man will abound with blessings, but whoever hastens to be rich will not go unpunished" (Proverbs 28:20, ESV).

Squandering shows our lack of faithfulness to God. To squander means to waste something, especially money, in a reckless or foolish manner. Luke 14:28-30 says this:

> "For which of you, desiring to build a tower, does not first sit down and count the cost, whether he has enough to complete it? Otherwise, when he has laid a foundation and is not able to finish, all who see it begin to mock him, saying, 'This man began to build and was not able to finish'" (ESV).

We waste God's provision with reckless and unprepared spending. It's God's money, not ours. If we want something, we can ask God. He's a good Father, and He will provide for our needs. He will also give us wisdom and strategies to do what He has given us to do without squandering.

When we talk about prodigals, we usually mean anyone who is lost—someone who is not in a relationship with the Lord. And yes, it means that. But the word "prodigal" literally means "squanderer." Someone who wastes money.

The prodigal son in Jesus' parable did two big things. First, he left his father's house, so he left his authority. He was not under authority any longer. Remember the Centurion? He had authority because he was under authority.[31] The prodigal was not under authority, so he had no authority. The second big thing the prodigal did was waste the money he got from his father. This is where he got his nickname; he spent foolishly.[32]

When we disobey God with our finances, we come out from under His authority. We then lose our authority. If we lose our authority with money, the next thing you know, we could be squandering it too. Is it possible to be a prodigal sitting right in church? We can't just pray for our money to do what God says it can do. We have to do with our money what God says so that our money comes under His authority. Evangelist Oral Roberts used to say, "God knows your financial need; what He needs is your seed."

DOING OUR PART

I've never seen a baby born with a suitcase, nor have I seen a hearse pulling a U-Haul. We come into the world with nothing, and we leave this world with nothing. It is ours for a short period of time to manage. First John 2:15-16 says:

> Do not love the world or anything in the world. If anyone loves the world, love for the Father is not in them. For everything in the world—the lust of the flesh, the lust of the eyes, and the pride of life—comes not from the Father but from the world (NIV).

We must love God more than we love what He has given us! We must love Him. In loving Him, we want to be good stewards of what He gives us, not for ourselves, but for His purpose. To be a good steward means doing our part. It means taking faith and combining it with the actions God asks of us. Some actions are easy to know because they are clear in the Bible. Other actions must be weighed with wisdom and revelation. But doing our part isn't to be compared to doing someone else's part. The important thing is that we know our part, and we do it. Just like David's men. Some fought and some stayed to rest and watch the supplies, but both got the same reward because they both did their part:

> David said to his men, "Each of you strap on your sword!" So they did, and David strapped his on as well. About four hundred men went up with David, while two hundred stayed with the supplies...Then David came to the two hundred men who had been too exhausted to follow him and who were left behind at the Besor Valley. They came out to meet David and the men with him. As David and his men approached, he asked them how they were. But all the evil men and troublemakers among David's followers said, "Because they did not go out with us, we will not share with them the plunder we recovered. However, each man may take his wife and children and go." David replied, "No, my brothers, you must not do that with what the Lord has given us. He has protected us and delivered into our hands the raiding party that came against us. Who will

listen to what you say? The share of the man who stayed with the supplies is to be the same as that of him who went down to the battle. All will share alike." David made this a statute and ordinance for Israel from that day to this (1 Samuel 25:13; 30:21-25, NIV).

David rewarded each soldier for what they were entrusted to do. The ones who stayed behind with the supplies got their reward because they did their part. The parable of the talents shows us that this same principle applies whether you have been given much or little. We must be faithful to do our part.

> "For it will be like a man going on a journey, who called his servants and entrusted to them his property. To one he gave five talents, to another two, to another one, to each according to his ability. Then he went away. He who had received the five talents went at once and traded with them, and he made five talents more. So also he who had the two talents made two talents more. But he who had received the one talent went and dug in the ground and hid his master's money...But his master answered him, 'You wicked and slothful servant! You knew that I reap where I have not sown and gather where I scattered no seed? Then you ought to have invested my money with the bankers, and at my coming I should have received what was my own with interest. So take the talent from him and give it to him who has the ten talents'" (Matthew 25:14-18; 26-28, ESV).

God cares that we manage our money well—that we sow and reap—that we do our part to be productive with our money.

It doesn't matter if you are on the front lines or if your part is to stay by the supplies. If you are too exhausted to fight, yet you are being faithful to what God has called you to do—being a good steward over the supplies, finances, and people God has asked you to oversee—then you get the same reward and blessings as those on the front line in battle. And if you are faithful, God promises you'll lack nothing,[33] that He will give you the power to create wealth,[34] prevent loss,[35] and supply all your needs.[36] It's all His anyway. You're just managing it.

PRAYER AND ACTIVATION

I encourage you to take a look at the last thirty days of transactions in your bank account. Many banks have easy ways to summarize these transactions, and there are several free websites and mobile phone applications that can summarize them for you also. As you look at the last thirty days, what story do your transactions tell? Can you see faithfulness in tithes and offerings? Can you see generosity in giving to others and meeting needs? What about investments that have the potential to create wealth (Deuteronomy 8:18)? Are there any patterns of squandering (wasting)?

Our bank transactions are deeds we have done with our finances. They show what we believe and where our faith actually is. If your bank transactions don't show you evidence of what you believe the Bible says about money, ask God to give you the grace to change that today. Simply repent if you haven't been obedient to His Word with your finances, and then just as Jesus told the woman at the well: go and sin no more.

Let's pray this prayer together:

Lord, thank You for trusting me with the finances You have given me. Thank You that it is You who gives the power to get wealth. Thank You for supplying all my needs. Thank You that because I obey You with tithes, You have shut the mouth of the devourer. Thank You for opportunities to give with a cheerful heart, to meet the needs of others, and to show Your generosity. And thank You for giving me strategies to multiply the resources You've given me in order that I can be a good and faithful steward over them all. In Jesus' name. Amen.

Endnotes:
[31]Matthew 8:8-9.
[32]Luke 15:11-32.
[33]Psalm 34:10.
[34]Deuteronomy 8:18.
[35]Malachi 3:10-12.
[36]Philippians 4:19.

Chapter 11

THE WORK OF OUR HANDS

While preaching a sermon recently, I asked the audience a question. To be clear, I don't speak publicly very often. I've spoken at churches and women's conferences, and even while pastoring for a while, but it's not my preference. But when I feel like God wants me to speak publicly, even though it's not something I am comfortable doing, I get out of my comfort zone to manage what God has asked me to do. So when I agreed to my sister-in-law Jane's request to speak on this topic of stewardship at Vision Church (Santa Rosa Beach, FL), I made my sermon as interactive as I could in order to keep some of the focus off of me. Smart, right?

The question I asked was this: "Whose church is this?" It's such a simple question, but there's a lot to think about. Is it our church as the congregation? We are the ones attending, volunteering, and tithing. Without us there is no church. So maybe it's our church. Or is it the pastors' church? Tom and Jane Hamon are the pastors. They make all the decisions. They do the speaking, hiring, and overseeing. They lead the weekly meetings. And if they left suddenly, the church would be in jeopardy. So, perhaps it is their church. But actually, they aren't even the ones who started the church or the worldwide ministry connected to it. Our dad, Dr. Hamon (known as Bishop to those who are part of the ministry), did. He is the founder. They are the pastors, but they are accountable to him. The church is under his ministry covering. So, is it Bishop Hamon's church?

I'm sure you already know the answer, but I'll spell it out for you. The church I attend is not my church. It is not the pastors' church. And it is not the founder's, denomination's, or covering ministry's church. It is God's church. And I would hope so—because I'm not going to that church otherwise! I don't want to be here if this is Pastor Tom and Jane's church or Bishop Hamon's ministry. If it isn't God's church, which God happened to put Tom and Jane Hamon as managers over, then I want no part of it. The same is true for your church.

Pastors frequently use the term "my people." But are the members of the congregation their people? In reality, they are responsible to manage the people, but the people don't belong to them. Ephesians 4:11 says their responsibility is to equip them for the work of the ministry. If the pastors are good managers, they'll equip God's people as though they are God's and not theirs. I come to my church because I know God is the God of my church. I know the pastor and founder are good managers. I know they're good and faithful servants. But I know they know it doesn't stop with them. They know that it is God's ministry. So do they have to worry about it? No. They just have to manage it. Talk about the load that takes off of them! The whole congregation is not the pastor's responsibility. Pastors just have to do the part God has given them to do.

Nothing is ours. What we do is not ours. Our job is not ours. Our church is not ours. Our work is not ours. It's God's. Colossians 3:17 says, "And whatever you do, whether in word or deed, do it all in the name of the Lord Jesus, giving thanks to God the Father through him" (NIV). Guess what? God puts His name on whatever we do as if He was the One doing it. So how do we do His work in His name?

WORKING FOR OUR INCOME OR CAREER

I've had some kind of job for most of my adult life. I've been a school bus driver and a bank teller. I worked in a sandwich shop. I worked for a temp agency, and I worked doing accounting for a business. And now I am the Chief Operating Officer of a ministry. Every job I had, other than my own business, I had to answer to a boss. I worked for him or her; I worked for their companies. I worked for their goals and visions. And I'm OK with that. I'm pretty good at settling in and doing my part. Maybe you are too.

Many of us do our jobs because, well, it's our job. We want the paycheck. We don't want to get fired. We want a promotion. Or we want some other perk for doing our jobs even better. There are lots of reasons to do our jobs and do them well. But what if I told you that your paycheck might be the least of your reasons for working? What if I told you that your employer is not even where you get your paycheck from anyway?

Before you put down this book thinking I'm crazy, hear me out. Your employer's name is on your paycheck. Someone in your company writes the check. Someone signs it. Someone delivers it to you. It comes out of the money earned by that company. If the company ran out of money, they might not give you a paycheck (unless they're insured to cover such a scenario). But even if that happened, your paycheck wouldn't have disappeared because of the company. It didn't come because of the company, and it won't go away because of the company. Your paycheck, and mine, come only from God. All provision does.

> Lifting up his eyes, then, and seeing that a large crowd was coming toward him, Jesus said to Philip, "Where are we to buy bread, so that these people may eat?" He said this to test him, for he himself knew what he would do. Philip answered him, "Two hundred denarii worth of bread would not be enough for each of them to get a little." One of his disciples, Andrew, Simon Peter's brother, said to him, "There is a boy here who has five barley loaves and two fish, but what are they for so many?" Jesus said, "Have the people sit down." Now there was much grass in the place. So the men sat down, about five thousand in number. Jesus then took the loaves, and when he had given thanks, he distributed them to those who were seated. So

also the fish, as much as they wanted. And when they had eaten their fill, he told his disciples, "Gather up the leftover fragments, that nothing may be lost." So they gathered them up and filled twelve baskets with fragments from the five barley loaves left by those who had eaten (John 6:5-13, ESV).

When they ran out of provision, even for five thousand, God provided. All provision comes from God.

So why do we think a paycheck is our biggest reason for working? Or why do we think promotion is the main reason to do more than the minimum? I know people who would quit their jobs this instant if they could afford it. I know some who hate their jobs, but say things like, "Oh well, everyone's got to make a living somehow." Or some decide after a disappointment, "I'll do what I was hired to do. But that's the last time I'll go above and beyond for them!" The sad thing is all these mindsets are hurting the employee. We can't make our decisions at work based on what we think we're getting in return from our employers. The only way to make the best decision and perform the best on our jobs is to have a biblical understanding about our jobs in the first place.

This can even be a struggle for those in ministry. I can remember my father telling me stories of getting almost nothing in an offering and believing God just for enough funds to get to the next place to preach. Then God would make up the difference at the next church we went to, or someone would come up and shake his hand and there would be money slipped to him. When you have a wife and three children traveling in ministry, you can't put your faith in the pastor or the congregation to provide for your family and give you a good offering. You have to trust and believe God will be your employer and take care of your needs.

I learned at a young age that only God can write my paycheck. It feels good sometimes to know that. It feels scary other times. I had to settle it for many reasons, one of which was that working for a church or ministry means relying largely on donations. When donations go dry, which they do at times, I still have bills to pay. I still need a paycheck. But it's not only true when things are tight. Even when the money seems limitless, my paycheck still doesn't come from the company whose name is on it. God and only God is our Provider.

So what is the truth about our jobs? It's in the Manual. Let's compare some common frustrations people face at work to what the Manual tells us.

FRUSTRATION: "I can't find a job that's right for me. I give up! God knows what job He has for me, so He will give it to me at the right time. He must not want me to work right now."

OK, so your latest job, or latest string of jobs, didn't feel like a good fit. What do you do with your time until you find the "right job" for you? The Bible is clear: "If anyone will not work, neither shall he eat" (2 Thessalonians 3:10, NKJV). A job that isn't right for us is better than no job at all.

FRUSTRATION: "My employers are unfair. They have passed me by for a promotion, even though I have been working here longer than the person they promoted. And the last person they hired makes the same amount of money I do. How can they do that? They don't appreciate me!"

I get it, it's tough not seeing the reward of your loyalty or feeling like someone else is getting valued more than you. Yet Matthew 20:8, 14 says, "Call the workers and pay them their wages, beginning with the last ones hired...I want to give the one who was hired last the same as I gave you" (NIV). Trust God to receive the paycheck He has for you. Even when our employers aren't making the best choices, we still honor God by how we serve them: "Servants, be subject to your masters with all respect, not only to the good and gentle but also to the unjust" (1 Peter 2:18, ESV).

FRUSTRATION: "My potential isn't being used at my job. They give me the go-fer work to do instead of letting me do what I'd be really good at. I could be more effective somewhere else."

OK. Maybe you have unused skills. However, your skill may not be the most important need at the moment. If your employer needs you to take out the trash, then taking out the trash is the most valuable thing you could do. Luke 16:10 says, "One who is faithful in a very little is also faithful in much, and one who is dishonest in a very little is also dishonest in much" (ESV). Even the woman whom Jesus referred to as a dog, though she may have been a great woman, was willing to be humble. Imagine the humility it took to deliver her response, "OK, but even the dogs get the scraps." Jesus was shocked at her faith, and her daughter was made whole from that very hour.[37]

Matthew 20:26 says, "Yet it shall not be so among you; but whoever desires to become great among you, let him be your servant" (NKJV). So if we're faithful in a few things, He'll make us ruler over many, and we will enter into the joy of the Lord. We want that, right? Have faith! Maybe taking out the trash is actually a pretty big step in becoming ruler over much at your workplace.

FRUSTRATION: "How do I know if God cares about my skill? I'm a hairdresser/graphic designer/auto mechanic/dog walker. What difference does that make to God?"

The old way of thinking was that God only cared about what's done inside the church building—preaching, worship leading, childcare, or maintenance to the building itself. But that idea came from dualism, a stem of false religion that teaches that natural things are not spiritual and that ultimately the natural and spiritual have nothing to do with each other. We know this just isn't true when we read the Scriptures:

"Do you see a man skillful in his work? He will stand before kings; he will not stand before obscure men" (Proverbs 22:29, ESV).

> The Lord said to Moses, "See, I have called by name Bezalel the son of Uri, son of Hur, of the tribe of Judah, and I have filled him with the Spirit of God, with ability and intelligence, with knowledge and all craftsmanship, to devise artistic designs, to work in gold, silver, and bronze, in cutting stones for setting, and in carving wood, to work in every craft" (Exodus 31:1-5, ESV).

Even Jesus was a carpenter and proved Himself faithful as a carpenter first before His public ministry. When God told Solomon to ask for anything he wanted, Solomon asked for wisdom to do the job God had given him to do. God was so pleased with that request, He gave Solomon wisdom and made him the richest man alive! God cares about your skill—your trade—your craft. He cares that you're excellent at it. He gave you the skills to do it in the first place! No matter what we do, we should do it in excellence as unto the Lord.

VOLUNTEERING AND SERVING

Working isn't only about what we do for an income. There are so many other areas where we also "work." Greeting at church is work. Making cookies for our kid's school fundraiser is work. Our duty to vote as Americans is work. Offering to do the dishes is work. Work just means this: activity involving mental or physical effort done in order to achieve a purpose or result. Well then, I don't know about you, but almost everything I do is work!

We usually call the kind of work we do without a paycheck "volunteering" or "serving." It's work. It benefits someone other than just ourselves. This work is just as important as the work we do for income. Colossians 3:23 says, "Whatever you do, work at it with all your heart, as working for the Lord, not for human masters" (NIV). Even if it seems like we are working for ourselves, we really aren't. We aren't even our own boss in our own homes. We're not even doing the dishes for ourselves. This verse says whatever we do is not for human masters. It's for the Lord. That means it matters. It can't be up to just our standards. It matters that it's up to His standards.

This is most obvious in our local churches. Any church has plenty of work that needs to be done. There's practical work like cutting grass, keeping things maintained, or making improvements. There's also meeting the needs of people who attend the church and meeting the needs of the community through the church. There are plenty of opportunities to work in any local church regardless of your skills or gifts.

Did you know local churches are considered the number one place to organize volunteers for community service outside the local church? Yeah, I was surprised to learn that, too. Volunteering generally is done so well at local churches that non-religious organizations look to churches to supply a volunteer force.[38] This means we're doing something right. We're fulfilling Matthew 5:16 which says, "In the same way, let your light shine before others, so that they may see your good works and give glory to your Father who is in heaven" (ESV).

But it isn't just some random "them" who participate in our churches. It isn't a group of people other than me and you. It is me. It is you. Each of us has a role to play in our local church. Ephesians 4:16 says, "From whom the whole body, joined and knit together by what every joint supplies, according to the effective working by which every part does its share, causes growth of the body for the edifying of itself in love" (NKJV). If we do not serve in our local churches, even if it's in the smallest thing, then we are not being the part of the Body God designed us to be.

I'm nearly the last person you'll see on the platform at my church, as I'm sure you have realized. Most of my family are ministers in some public way in our church. I don't. I don't preach (and rarely speak). I don't sing on the worship team. I don't teach children's church. But I'm still a minister in my church. I already know the place God has for me in my church. It's a background role. I take care of needs that the founder has. I'm a critical part of my family's ministry, even though a stranger or newcomer who walked into our church would have no idea. I minister to my family and my church by serving them. I'm doing what I know God has called me to do. I don't feel less than. Actually my family calls me their air traffic controller. If I didn't do what I do, there would be mass chaos. They would not be able to do what they do. I'm just like those soldiers of David's who stayed with the supplies and got the same reward. And for many of you, that should be you, too. As long as you are doing what you know God called you to do, you're being a good manager.

So back to the question I asked during my sermon at Vision Church CI, "Whose church is it?". It challenged me all right. Not because I didn't know the answer from the Bible, but because I had to ask myself if I was living the way I knew to live. Am I living out the answer I know from the Bible? Am I doing everything I do as though it's God's? Is my work God's? Are my hobbies God's? Is everything—every single thing—that I do done as unto the Lord?

I still ask myself this question. It's part of staying a good and faithful steward. If we manage our work well, as unto the Lord, God promises to make us rulers over much. It's all His. We're just managing.

PRAYER AND ACTIVATION

Take a minute to really ask yourself the above question, too. Are you doing everything you do as though that thing is God's: your work for income (if you have a job), your work at home, your hobbies, your volunteering, and anything else you do?

Let's pray this prayer together:

Lord, I acknowledge that nothing I do is ever outside of Your view. I don't do some things for You and some things for me. It's all for You, Lord. So for any area that I have taken ownership of and acted unto myself, I ask You to forgive me now, and I submit that area back to Your dominion. Thank You for reminding me today and every day that whatever I am doing is for You—even in the mundane things, even when I think what I'm doing doesn't matter, especially when I think it doesn't matter. Thank You for giving me the ability to do everything for Your glory and become a good and faithful steward of the work of my hands. In Jesus' name. Amen.

Endnotes:

[37]Matthew 15:27.

[38]Lipp, J. L. (2009). The Complete Idiots Guide to Recruiting and Managing Volunteers. New York: Alpha.

Chapter 12

STEWARDING OUR SOULS

I think by now we're all OK with the idea that everything we own and do is God's. Physically, we're God's. Mentally, we're God's. Spiritually, we're God's. But our feelings...those are ours, right? I mean I can't help the way I feel. I can't control my feelings. Is that even healthy? Well, I guess it depends on what the Manual says.

Emotions aren't just human; they come from God. He has emotions, too. He has compassion.[39] He gets angry.[40] He has joy and laughs.[41] He grieves.[42] He pities.[43] He loves.[44] He does things with His whole heart and soul.[45] God is all in. He is not without feelings or just serious. He's alive, and He made us in His image with a wide array of expressions and feelings. And since they all belong to Him, we ought to steward them the way He would in all areas of our lives. Let's look at some biblical ways to steward our souls.

RELATIONSHIPS AND LOVE

The first step to stewarding our souls is learning to love. Love is expressed in relationships. God wants us to have healthy relationships, so He gave us instructions about how to steward them well for them to be pleasing and productive. Being good stewards of relationships starts with being good stewards of our own emotions and reactions.

This is a good time to remember one of the biggest reasons God gives us relationships. It's not just so we won't be lonely. It's not just so we have someone to give to and serve. It's not just so we can reproduce (if we're married). It's not just so we can have an example of what He is like. The big thing it's really about is what the Bible says is all of our destinies. The biggest reason for relationships is to help us be conformed to the image of Christ.[46] This means we have a responsibility. There is responsibility in every relationship. To have a true relationship with someone, you covenant with them. When we got saved and gave our lives mentally, physically, and emotionally over to God, we took on the responsibility to become Christ-like. Remember God always gives you a choice on how you will manage what He has given you in your life, including relationships.

That's where love comes in. God is love, and He expects us to love. Good news, though! We can do this because love is a choice. If it wasn't, God wouldn't command us to love. A lot of people think, "I didn't mean to fall in love," or "you don't get to choose who you love." That just isn't true. Love is a choice. It's a lot of little choices, over and over again. What is God's description of love?

> Love is very patient and kind, never jealous or
> envious, never boastful or proud, never haughty
> or selfish or rude. Love does not demand its
> own way. It is not irritable or touchy. It does
> not hold grudges and will hardly even notice
> when others do it wrong. It is never glad about
> injustice, but rejoices whenever truth wins out.
> If you love someone, you will be loyal to him
> no matter what the cost. You will always
> believe in him, always expect the best of him,
> and always stand your ground in defending him
> (1 Corinthians 13:4-7, TLB).

These choices add up to love—not the feelings of desiring someone—not the joy we have. Those all come from love, but love first comes from making a choice.

God commands us to make that choice with everyone—even with our enemies. He specifically tells us to love our enemies and those who spitefully use us. You might be thinking, "Certainly God doesn't tell me who to love?" Yes, He does, because our emotions aren't ours. They're His! And if every relationship is helping us be conformed to the image of Christ, then maybe we don't have any true enemies. Joseph told his brothers, who sold Him into slavery, that God did this for His purpose. Even our enemies help us to be conformed to the image of Christ. James 1:2-4 says:

> Consider it a sheer gift, friends, when tests and
> challenges come at you from all sides. You
> know that under pressure, your faith-life is
> forced into the open and shows its true colors.
> So don't try to get out of anything prematurely.

Let it do its work so you become mature and well-developed, not deficient in any way (MSG).

So according to this Scripture in The Message Bible, tests and challenges are working for us. "For our light affliction, which is but for a moment, worketh for us a far more exceeding and eternal weight of glory" (2 Corinthians 4:17). We become mature and well-developed (Christ-like). By choosing to love others like the Manual says, we're fulfilling our destinies. God tells us to love our neighbors. He tells us to love ourselves. He tells husbands to love their wives as Christ loved the Church (His bride).

Maybe the easiest way to know if we are properly managing our relationships is to ask ourselves if we are being Christ-like and like Christ to the other person.

FORGIVENESS

God requires us to forgive indefinitely. He doesn't let us hold a grudge or sit and mull over our anger. We can't brood and stew and let our frustrations fester. We also can't just "vent" them to anyone to make ourselves feel better for a little while. We have to forgive. "For if you forgive men their trespasses, your heavenly Father will also forgive you" (Matthew 6:14, NKJV). Wait, what? "What if I don't like that? What if I feel like I can't forgive that person?" OK, well then your heavenly Father won't forgive you. Simple.

God doesn't require us to forgive just for the other person's sake; He requires us to forgive for our sake.

Medical studies have shown the effect bitterness and unforgiveness have on our bodies and souls. Ephesians 4:31-32 says, "Get rid of all bitterness, rage and anger, brawling and slander, along with every form of malice. Be kind and compassionate to one another, forgiving each other, just as in Christ God forgave you" (NIV).

Forgiveness is a choice just like love is. Even if we don't feel it, we have to choose to forgive. It starts in our will. Eventually, if we keep choosing to forgive, our hearts will change. The pain will lessen. The anger resolves. And even though the person may have done wrong, we are free because we have forgiven.

We also need to give people permission to be themselves. We're talking about management. People are managing their lives and what God has given them. Everyone has a different management style. My staff see a difference between my management style and my brother Tim's. We're different, but we're both good at what we're doing: using the skills and strengths God has given us and answering to God by obeying what He tells us. We both are being good stewards.

Even if someone is doing something differently than you, assume the best about them. Believe he or she is doing what God called him to do to the best of his ability, just like you're doing what God called you to do to the best of your ability. A lot of offenses can be avoided in the first place when we believe the best about each other. Sometimes people are not right or wrong, just different. If you have ever taken a personality profile or taken the "love languages" test, you will realize people can react very differently in the very same situation. Both may be correct, just different.

WORRY/ANXIETY

Matthew 6:25, 34 says:

> "Therefore I say to you, do not worry about your life, what you will eat or what you will drink; nor about your body, what you will put on. Is not life more than food and the body more than clothing?...Therefore do not worry about tomorrow, for tomorrow will worry about its own things" (NKJV).

Look, even the birds are flying around in the air without care. They're not worried. I picture Jesus shaking His head thinking, *"What is wrong with you? You're better than a bird!"* We're valuable to God, so why worry?

Some people worry about everything. It's like they think they have to worry: "I have to worry about what's going to happen tomorrow. I've got to worry about my kids. I have to worry about my health. What would happen if I didn't worry? I must worry about that too!" But why? It's not even theirs to worry about. And God commands us not to worry. Worry and being anxious doesn't change our situations; it doesn't fix anything. Prayer and faith will change our circumstances and can fix our problems.

Maybe one reason God doesn't want us to worry is because He knows that worry affects our souls.

> Be anxious for nothing, but in everything by prayer and supplication, with thanksgiving, let your requests be made known to God; and the peace of God, which surpasses all understanding, will guard your hearts and minds through Christ Jesus (Philippians 4:6-7, NKJV).

Worry is the opposite of the peace of God ruling our hearts. And the kingdom of God is righteousness, peace, and joy.[47] I don't know about you, but it's hard for me to have joy and worry at the same time.

To take good care of our souls, we have to trade worry for trust. Trust in God. Trust in His goodness. Worry is a lack of faith and trust in the Manual/Bible God has given us and a lack of faith and trust in our Creator, our Lord Jesus Christ. Trading worry for trust means giving Him permission to be God for us—not taking ownership of the things we're worried about. Remember, if we own it, then the buck stops with us. If God owns it, then He is ultimately responsible. If we take possession of our lives, then we take possession and lordship away from God, and we are responsible for our lives, not God. He will do His part. We don't own anything. We just manage what God gives us to manage, and trust Him to take care of the rest.

JOY AND PEACE

The joy of the Lord is our strength. "Laughter doeth good like a medicine" (Proverbs 17:22). Our having joy and peace is very important to the Lord. If we are weary and sad, it's because we are not trusting God. We are carrying our own burdens and being weighed down. Laughter is contagious. If one person begins to laugh, then normally others will follow. Paul says in Scripture to rejoice in the Lord always (Philippians 3:1 and 4:4). That means we are to celebrate. Let go of the burden. Have joy and peace. God says He will give us the desires of our hearts. God is a good Father. He wants His children to be happy. I get great pleasure seeing my children and grandchildren happy, laughing, and at peace. So does our Father.

ANGER

Anger is not a sin. It's an emotion we have, just like God has it. But the Bible says, "Be angry, and do not sin" (Ephesians 4:26, NKJV), which means anger can lead to sin. We can get a little mad every now and then. But we better not sin. And we better not let the sun go down on our wrath. We have to do the right thing with anger when it shows up. To forgive is one thing we can do. Another is to resolve it. Deal with anger quickly.

MURMURING AND COMPLAINING

The Israelites could not enter into their Promised Land (into the best God had for them) because of their murmuring and complaining according to Numbers 14. First Corinthians 10:10 says, "Neither murmur ye, as some of them also murmured, and were destroyed of the destroyer." What you say, the way you say it, and your motive and attitude behind it can keep you from God's best. Let's look at these Scriptures:

"Whoso keepeth his mouth and his tongue keepeth his soul from troubles" (Proverbs 21:23).

"Do all things without murmurings and disputings" (Philippians 2:14).

"O generation of vipers, how can ye, being evil, speak good things? for out of the abundance of the heart the mouth speaketh" (Matthew 12:34).

We must be good stewards of our mouths. What we say can affect our lives.

> When we put bits into the mouths of horses to make them obey us, we can turn the whole animal. Or take ships as an example. Although they are so large and are driven by strong winds, they are steered by a very small rudder wherever the pilot wants to go. Likewise, the tongue is a small part of the body, but it makes great boasts. Consider what a great forest is set on fire by a small spark. The tongue also is a fire, a world of evil among the parts of the body. It corrupts the whole body, sets the whole course of one's life on fire, and is itself set on fire by hell (James 3:3-6, NIV).

"God forbid: yea, let God be true, but every man a liar; as it is written, That thou mightest be justified in thy sayings, and mightest overcome when thou art judged. You are justified by your words" (Romans 3:4).

REST

I bet you didn't expect to see rest here. Resting is an important way to be a good steward of the soul God gave us. On the seventh day of creation, God rested. If God needs rest, we need rest. And He wants us to have it. There is an old saying: "Come apart to rest awhile before you come apart." Just look at these Scriptures:

"And he said, 'My presence will go with you, and I will give you rest'" (Exodus 33:14, ESV).

"And he said to them, 'Come away by yourselves to a desolate place and rest a while.' For many were coming and going, and they had no leisure even to eat" (Mark 6:31, ESV).

"For thus said the Lord God, the Holy One of Israel, 'In returning and rest you shall be saved; in quietness and in trust shall be your strength'" (Isaiah 30:15, ESV).

"A promise remains of entering His rest" (Hebrews 4:1, NKJV).

"For I will satisfy the weary soul, and every languishing soul I will replenish" (Jeremiah 31:25, ESV).

"The Lord is my shepherd; I shall not want. He makes me lie down in green pastures. He leads me beside still waters. He restores my soul" (Psalm 23:1-2, ESV).

Rest is natural and emotional:

"Come to me, all who labor and are heavy laden, and I will give you rest. Take my yoke upon you, and learn from me, for I am gentle and lowly in heart, and you will find rest for your souls. For my yoke is easy, and my burden is light" (Matthew 11:28-30, ESV).

Rest means both giving ourselves time to have natural rest as well as choosing to be at rest in our emotions, knowing He carries the burden.

Counselors tell us that emotions are not right or wrong, just real. But even emotions belong to God. Just like our thoughts, we may have emotions we didn't choose. But once they show up, we choose what we do about them. I've also heard it said this way: "It's OK to not be OK. It's just not OK to stay that way." Four essentials for natural and spiritual health and growth are eat, drink, exercise, and rest.

God tells us in the Manual exactly what to do. If we don't worry. If we don't get angry and sin. If we love our neighbor. If we love our enemy. If we love ourselves. If we take care of our family and our relationships. If we don't have doubt and unbelief. And if we believe in Him and trust Him, we can be good, faithful, and trustworthy servants. Our emotions and our souls will line up when we do what the Bible says. We don't have to worry about depression. We don't have to worry about anger. We don't have to worry about fear and doubt. We don't have to worry at all, since He will watch over our souls.

If we cast our cares on Him, forgive, let go of anger, and choose joy and peace, He promises to work all things out for our good. We're choosing His character so He can make us into His image. Our souls are His anyway. We're just managers.

PRAYER AND ACTIVATION

All areas listed above are critical for being good stewards of our souls. Perhaps the most crucial, though, is the area of forgiveness. The Bible is clear that if we do not forgive others, God cannot forgive us. Many Christians do not fully forgive the way Jesus forgives. This is detrimental. If we haven't forgiven from our hearts, what other good can we really do for our souls?

Take a minute and ask the Lord to show you if there is anyone you may need to forgive. Even if you feel you have forgiven that person 100 times for the wrong they did, if there's even the slightest wince in your heart about how he or she wronged you, go ahead and forgive them again.

Once you have worked through any forgiveness God shows you, pray with me:

Lord, make me a good steward of the soul You have given me. My soul yearns and even faints for Your presence, Lord. My heart and flesh cry out for You. Instead of shame, You give double honor. So Lord, as I have forgiven others, and as You have forgiven me, I ask You to fill my soul with every good thing You have—with joy, peace, hope, and strength. You resist the proud, but You give grace to the humble. I humble myself and yield to You, asking for Your presence to touch my heart and restore my soul. In Jesus' name. Amen.

Now, I encourage you to spend at least thirty minutes praying in tongues today. You can do this every day. When you pray in tongues, you build yourself up. What a great gift to use as we steward our souls well!

Endnotes:

[39]Psalm 103:13; Exodus 33:19; Isaiah 30:18; James 5:11; Lamentations 3:32; 2 Corinthians 1:3-4; Matthew 9:35-38; Mark 6:30-44; Luke 15:11-32.

[40]Deuteronomy 9:8; Exodus 15:7; Job 4:9; Jeremiah 32:29; Lamentations 2:2; Numbers 32:13; Habakkuk 3:12; Isaiah 13:9.

[41]Isaiah 62:5; Jeremiah 32:41; Zephaniah 3:17; Psalm 2:4; 37:13; Proverbs 1:26.

[42]Genesis 6:6; Psalm 78:40.

[43]Judges 2:18.

[44]Jeremiah 31:3.

[45]Jeremiah 32:41.

[46]Romans 8:28-29.

[47]Romans 14:17.

AFTERWORD
by Sherilyn Hamon-Miller

At the time of writing this book, I'm the COO of a world-wide ministry organization whose leaders and members are primarily known for their good character and integrity. That means a lot to me. I didn't set out for this job, but I arrived here naturally after nearly a decade of applying the principles in this book. But you know what the best part is? The best part is that it's not just about me; it's about the Body of Christ. It's about how each of us fits into the Body of Christ and impacts one another. It's about the fact that by stewarding my life well, I may be able to affect you positively, even though we may have never even met.

Our bigger impact is really what matters, isn't it? I imagine you don't just want to succeed. You want your success to matter. You want it to make a difference in someone else's life. Well, I have good news. When your life fits rightly into its role in the earth, the whole Body of Christ benefits. This is what Paul says about us as one Body:

> Until we all attain to the unity of the faith and of the knowledge of the Son of God, to mature manhood, to the measure of the stature of the fullness of Christ, so that we may no longer be children, tossed to and fro by the waves and carried about by every wind of doctrine, by human cunning, by craftiness in deceitful schemes. Rather, speaking the truth in love, we are to grow up in every way into him who is the head, into Christ, from whom the whole body, joined and held together by every joint with which it is equipped, when each part is working properly, makes the body grow so that it builds itself up in love (Ephesians 4:13-16, ESV).

See, we don't just have our own individual purposes. We have a corporate purpose as the worldwide Body of Christ. Isn't that amazing? And in order for that Body to grow up, according to this Scripture, each of us has to supply what we are meant to supply.

This is exciting news. It means that no matter what you are called to do—whether you're a minister, or a bank teller, or a stay-at-home parent—you are making an impact on every believer! You are valuable. Who you become, the quality of your character, everything you do is all valuable.

So what do we do next? We can't make ourselves perfect. We can't work on everything at once. As we become aware of our lives and how well we're managing, we will notice our ups and downs. Some days we will manage an area well; some days we may not. We might even forget to evaluate our management in the first place. The important thing is that we become willing, become aware, and do our best.

I pray this book has inspired you to be willing to better manage every aspect of your life. Knowing the impact that managing your life well will have on your own life will help make you willing. Knowing the impact that managing well will have on the Body of Christ will help, too.

Right now, while it's on your mind, you'll naturally become more aware of your management. But you can also do some things to help make you aware. Ask the Holy Spirit to make you aware each day of an area you're managing. He'll nudge you. John 13:16 says that He will guide you in all truth—that includes this truth. And then do your best. Your best may not be the same as someone else's best. Your best probably won't be perfect either. But do your best anyway. As you do, your best will also improve.

I recommend picking one area to evaluate and work on at a time. God may already be highlighting an area to you. Try making a list of behaviors, responsibilities, or expectations in that area and start with improving just one. You can use the chapters in this book as your reference.

Managing well is not a one-time fix. It's a lifetime of accountability with yourself and the Holy Spirit. We will never be done being good and faithful servants or wise stewards. That's why building awareness of our management is so valuable. That skill will serve you for the rest of your life, and maybe even in eternity.

The more you become aware of your management, the more you will be able to choose to be good, faithful, and wise. The better you manage, the more you'll live your best life and the better you'll fit in your role in the Body of Christ. The better you are, the better the world will become—all because you stewarded your life well!

ABOUT THE AUTHOR

 **SHERILYN HAMON-MILLER** serves Christian International as the Chief Operating Officer and corporate secretary. She is the Administrator and personal assistant to Bishop Bill Hamon. Sherilyn has held many different responsibilities throughout her life, including pastoring for 10 years, traveling in full-time ministry for 10 years, owning her own business, and working for several different businesses. She is also a mother, but her favorite job is Gramma! Sherilyn is the only daughter of Drs. Bill and Evelyn Hamon. She lives in Santa Rosa Beach, Florida and has four children, three children-in-law, and five beautiful grandchildren.

CONTACT INFORMATION

SHERILYN HAMON-MILLER:
GoodandFaithfulSteward4.2@gmail.com.

CHRISTIAN INTERNATIONAL:
(800)388-5308